on
london

Dickens
on
london

ET REMOTISSIMA PROPE

'on'

'on'
Published by Hesperus Press Limited
4 Rickett Street, London sw6 1RU
www.hesperuspress.com

'Gin Shops' first published in *The Evening Chronicle*, 1835
'Scotland Yard' first published in *The Morning Chronicle*, 1836
'Seven Dials' first published in *Bell's Life in London*, 1837
'Heart of London' and 'The Giant Chronicles' first published in *Master Humphrey's Clock*, 1843
'Gone Astray' first published in *Household Words*, 1853
'Night Walks' and 'City of the Absent' first published in 'The Uncommercial Traveller series' in *All the Year Round*, 1860 and 1863
This collection first published by Hesperus Press Limited, 2010

Introduction © Pete Orford, 2010
Selection © Hesperus Press Limited, 2010

Designed and typeset by Fraser Muggeridge studio
Printed in Jordan by Al-Khayyam Printing Press

ISBN: 978-1-84391-615-4

Contents

Introduction   vii

On London   1
   The Heart of London   3
   Gone Astray   7
   Scotland Yard   21
   Seven Dials   27
   Gin-Shops   33
   City of the Absent   39
   The Giant Chronicles   49
   Night Walks   71

Notes   81

Biographical note   83

Introduction

Charles Dickens without London simply would not have been Charles Dickens. The city provided the writer with a constant source of material, bursting with vitality, vice, people of all types and, most importantly, stories. London was his muse, providing real locations in which to ground his fictional adventures, but moreover inspiring and challenging him as an author; the vast metropolis provided both opportunity for stories and adventure, which appealed to Dickens, whilst also confronting his idealistic view of the world with regular scenes of crime, poverty and deprivation – London forced Dickens to grow up.

It was a major part not only of his writing, but of his day-to-day life. He first moved to the city when he was three years old, and aside from five years in Chatham he then stayed in London until he was forty-four. The city thus provided him with life experience, from his infamous and shame-ridden childhood work at Warren's blacking factory through his early career as a solicitor's clerk and parliamentary reporter, before he found his vocation as an author and editor. Much has been said, perhaps too much, on the importance of the blacking factory and its influence on the young Dickens, but one thing that it certainly demonstrates is the capacity for life in the city to forcefully intrude on the ideals of the child. Consequently, in the writings collected here we can see the contrast between moments of wide-eyed wonder and cynical observation; just as London could offer both architectural wonders and slums, big businessmen and beggars, monarchy and murderers, so too we can see in Dickens the schism of optimist and pessimist. He sees both the best in people and the worst in people. He writes about the horrors and wrong-doings of society, whilst also retreating into his own fantastic view of the world around him.

This sense of the fantastic in Dickens can be seen in the way he anthropomorphises London. For Dickens, the city was much more than bricks and mortar; it was a living organism with its own personality and opinions; a sentient being taking a careful watch over its brood of inhabitants. In the extract from *Master Humphrey's Clock*, 'The Heart of London' (1841), Dickens shows the city as a mother caring for its inhabitants, the author pleading in addition that those inhabitants care for each other as a family. In many ways this sets out the divide in the city as Dickens saw it – the glory of London marred by the negligence of its poorer citizens.

It is interesting therefore to see the views of the younger Dickens explored in 'Gone Astray' (1853); the older writer's recounting of his childhood view of London reveals that he was fascinated with the city from an early age, observing the people around him and responding to inanimate objects as living counterparts who watch him, talk to him and have their own stories to tell. He acknowledges his own love of fantasy and imagination, suggesting that the trip to London is initially made 'to quench [his] romantic fire, and bring [him] to a practical state' by showing him the reality behind the city of his childhood stories. The child confuses fact with fiction and thus explores London as a place of high adventure, with Sinbad the sailor and giants lurking round the corner; the adult Dickens wonders at the naivety of his younger self whilst mourning that loss of innocence.

As he matured, Dickens balanced his imaginative view of the world around him with his growing awareness of injustice and depravity in the city. His early writings under the pseudonym of Boz are a combination of sombre reflection and comic invention. In 'Gin Shops' (1835) and 'Scotland Yard' (1836), he sneers at the shallowness of revamping traditional areas into trendy metropolitan sites, while both here and in 'Seven Dials' (1837) he alternates between championing the vitality of the people, and pitying their deplorable lives or criticising the vicious aspects of their characters as formed by their upbringing and environment. He often finds himself torn between laughing at and pitying his fellow Londoners; the wide-eyed childhood view he carried with him both detached him from his peers and encouraged him to embrace them. He admired the mass, but often criticised the individual.

But it's also important to remember that for all his good intentions, Dickens was nonetheless using all of these observations to make his own fame and fortune. The articles for *Sketches by Boz* were just the first of many he would write about London and its people, using them as a ready source of material for comedy, both factual and fictionalised. For all his discourses on the wrongs of man, the storywriter in Dickens was always prevalent and continuously we can see how he imbues the everyday with the fantastic; in 'City of the Absent' (1863) he takes the humdrum environment of the abandoned churchyards in London, and shows the potential they have as areas of life, love and despair. His triumph is in showing each reader the wonders of the urban world that they had previously taken for granted.

Dickens' colourful account of the everyday paves the way for his fiction work, and in 'The Giant Chronicles' (1840) we can see how his knowledge of and love for London combine with his storytelling ability. The Chronicles were originally planned to be a series, occurring sporadically in *Master Humphrey's Clock*, but dwindling figures led Dickens to change his approach to the journal and focus on longer narratives instead. Accordingly, we only have the introduction to the Chronicles and the first tale, which offers an idea of what Dickens might have done had he been free to pursue his original plan of telling stories from the city's past. The giants telling the Chronicles are those who he saw and wondered at in 'Gone Astray'; the idea of city genii or guardian spirits watching over London's citizens resonates with 'The Heart of London'; his character types and crowd scenes are built upon his sketches written under the pseudonym of Boz. In this tale, Dickens literally uses the city as inspiration, making it the focal point of the Chronicles. Joe Toddyhigh, the chronicler, is initially disillusioned with the city, thinking 'that London was a dreary, desolate place'; yet his encounters with the giants (had they continued) promise to enlighten him to the wonders held within the metropolis. It embodies the city's hold on Dickens' writing as a well of inspiration, prompting stories, ideas and characters.

As a child and young man Dickens wondered at the metropolis, revelling in its eccentricities; but with age, inevitably, he became more jaded, and this attitude spills over into his writing. In 'Night Walks' (1860), in which he describes a number of nocturnal excursions he pursued following the death of his father, Dickens broods on the dark soul of the city. Where the child stood agog and looked for Sinbad and giants, the adult Dickens shuns society, peering into theatres after the audience has left, encountering drunks and wandering the streets with thoughts of crime and sin. Even here, though, while he focuses on the grittier side of the city, Dickens' fantasising shines through, romanticising the desolate scenes with suggestions of magic and wonder. He 'knew well enough where to find vice and misfortune of all kinds, if [he] had chosen; but they were put out of sight'; he both acknowledges and shuns the dark heart of London. His love of the city was not born of naivety; he was fully aware of the horrors in London, and accepted the city despite them, not in ignorance of them. Ultimately what we can take from Dickens' relationship with London is a number of works responding to the writer's immediate environment, a man's attempt to reconcile the everyday with his own imaginative pursuits, to counter his observations of depravity with his faith in humanity.

– Pete Orford, 2010

On London

The Heart of London

There came towards us upon the wind the voice of the deep and distant bell of St Paul's as it struck the hour of midnight. I had seen it but a few days before, and could not help telling of the fancy I had had about it.

I paid my fee of twopence, upon entering, to one of the money-changers who sit within the Temple; and falling, after a few turns up and down, into the quiet train of thought which such a place awakens, paced the echoing stones like some old monk whose present world lay all within its walls. As I looked afar up into the lofty dome, I could not help wondering what were his reflections whose genius reared that mighty pile, when, the last small wedge of timber fixed, the last nail driven into its home for many centuries, the clang of hammers and the hum of busy voices gone, and the great silence whole years of noise had helped to make, reigning undisturbed around, he mused, as I did now, upon his work, and lost himself amid its vast extent. I could not quite determine whether the contemplation of it would impress him with a sense of greatness or of insignificance; but when I remembered how long a time it had taken to erect, in how short a space it might be traversed even to its remotest parts, for how brief a term he, or any of those who cared to bear his name, would live to see it, or know of its existence, I imagined him far more melancholy than proud, and looking with regret upon his labour done. With these thoughts in my mind, I began to ascend, almost unconsciously, the flight of steps leading to the several wonders of the building, and found myself before a barrier where another money-taker sat, who demanded which among them I would choose to see. There were the stone gallery, he said, and the whispering gallery, the geometrical staircase, the room of models, the clock – the clock being quite in my way, I stopped him there, and chose that sight from all the rest.

I groped my way into the turret which it occupies, and saw before me, in a kind of loft, what seemed to be a great, old oaken press with folding doors. These being thrown back by the attendant (who was sleeping when I came upon him, and looked a drowsy fellow, as though his close companionship with Time had made him quite indifferent to it), disclosed a complicated crowd of wheels and chains in iron and brass – great, sturdy, rattling engines – suggestive of breaking a finger put in here or there, and grinding the bone to powder – and these were the clock! Its very pulse, if I may use the word, was like no other clock. It did not mark the flight of every moment with a gentle second stroke, as though it would check old Time, and have him stay his pace in pity, but measured it with one sledge-hammer beat, as if its business were to crush the seconds as they came trooping on, and remorselessly to clear a path before the day of judgment.

I sat down opposite it, and hearing its regular and never-changing voice, that one deep constant note, uppermost amongst all the noise and clatter in the streets below – marking that, let that tumult rise or fall, go on or stop – let it be night or noon, tomorrow or today, this year or next – it still performed its functions with the same dull constancy, and regulated the progress of the life around, the fancy came upon me that this was London's heart, and that when it should cease to beat, the city would be no more.

It is night. Calm and unmoved amidst the scenes that darkness favours, the great heart of London throbs in its giant breast. Wealth and beggary, vice and virtue, guilt and innocence, repletion and the direst hunger, all treading on each other and crowding together, are gathered round it. Draw but a little circle above the clustering housetops, and you shall have within its space everything, with its opposite extreme and contradiction, close beside. Where yonder feeble light is shining a man is but this moment dead. The taper at a few yards' distance is seen by eyes that have this instant opened on the world. There are two houses

4

separated by but an inch or two of wall. In one, there are quiet minds at rest; in the other, a waking conscience that one might think would trouble the very air. In that close corner where the roofs shrink down and cower together, as if to hide their secrets from the handsome street hard by, there are such dark crimes, such miseries and horrors, as could be hardly told in whispers. In the handsome street, there are folks asleep who have dwelt there all their lives, and have no more knowledge of these things than if they had never been, or were transacted at the remotest limits of the world – who, if they were hinted at, would shake their heads, look wise, and frown, and say they were impossible, and out of nature – as if all great towns were not. Does not this heart of London, that nothing moves, nor stops, nor quickens – that goes on the same let what will be done – does it not express the city's character well?

The day begins to break, and soon there is the hum and noise of life. Those who have spent the night on doorsteps and cold stones crawl off to beg; they who have slept in beds come forth to their occupation too, and business is astir. The fog of sleep rolls slowly off, and London shines awake. The streets are filled with carriages and people gaily clad. The jails are full, too, to the throat; nor have the workhouses or hospitals much room to spare.

The courts of law are crowded. Taverns have their regular frequenters by this time, and every mart of traffic has its throng. Each of these places is a world, and has its own inhabitants; each is distinct from, and almost unconscious of the existence of any other. There are some few people well to do, who remember to have heard it said, that numbers of men and women – thousands, they think it was – get up in London every day, unknowing where to lay their heads at night; and that there are quarters of the town where misery and famine always are. They don't believe it quite – there may be some truth in it, but it is exaggerated, of course. So, each of these thousand worlds goes on, intent upon itself, until night comes again – first with its lights and pleasures, and its cheerful streets; then with its guilt and darkness.

Heart of London, there is a moral in thy every stroke! As I look on at thy indomitable working, which neither death, nor press of life, nor grief, nor gladness out of doors will influence one jot, I seem to hear a voice within thee which sinks into my heart, bidding me, as I elbow my way among the crowd, have some thought for the meanest wretch that passes, and, being a man, to turn away with scorn and pride from none that bear the human shape.

Gone Astray

When I was a very small boy indeed, both in years and stature, I got lost one day in the city of London. I was taken out by Somebody (shade of Somebody forgive me for remembering no more of thy identity!), as an immense treat, to be shown the outside of St Giles' Church. I had romantic ideas in connection with that religious edifice; firmly believing that all the beggars who pretended through the week to be blind, lame, one-armed, deaf and dumb, and otherwise physically afflicted, laid aside their pretences every Sunday, dressed themselves in holiday clothes, and attended divine service in the temple of their patron saint. I had a general idea that the reigning successor of Bampfylde Moore Carew[1] acted as a sort of churchwarden on these occasions, and sat in a high pew with red curtains.

It was in the spring-time when these tender notions of mine, bursting forth into new shoots under the influence of the season, became sufficiently troublesome to my parents and guardians to occasion Somebody to volunteer to take me to see the outside of St Giles' Church, which was considered likely (I suppose) to quench my romantic fire, and bring me to a practical state. We set off after breakfast. I have an impression that Somebody was got up in a striking manner – in cord breeches of fine texture and milky hue, in long jean gaiters, in a green coat with bright buttons, in a blue neckerchief, and a monstrous shirt-collar. I think he must have newly come (as I had myself) out of the hop-grounds of Kent. I considered him the glass of fashion and the mould of form: a very Hamlet without the burden of his difficult family affairs.

We were conversational together, and saw the outside of St Giles' Church with sentiments of satisfaction, much enhanced by a flag flying from the steeple. I infer that we then went down to Northumberland House in the Strand to view the celebrated lion over the gateway. At all events, I know that in the act of looking up with mingled awe and admiration at that famous animal I lost Somebody.

The child's unreasoning terror of being lost, comes as freshly on me now as it did then. I verily believe that if I had found myself astray at the North Pole instead of in the narrow, crowded, inconvenient street over which the lion in those days presided, I could not have been more horrified. But this first fright expended itself in a little crying and tearing up and down; and then I walked, with a feeling of dismal dignity upon me, into a court, and sat down on a step to consider how to get through life.

To the best of my belief, the idea of asking my way home never came into my head. It is possible that I may, for the time, have preferred the dismal dignity of being lost; but I have a serious conviction that in the wide scope of my arrangements for the future, I had no eyes for the nearest and most obvious course. I was but very juvenile; from eight to nine years old, I fancy.

I had one and fourpence in my pocket, and a pewter ring with a bit of red glass in it on my little finger. This jewel had been presented to me by the object of my affections, on my birthday, when we had sworn to marry, but had foreseen family obstacles to our union, in her being (she was six years old) of the Wesleyan persuasion, while I was devotedly attached to the Church of England. The one and fourpence were the remains of half-a-crown, presented on the same anniversary by my godfather – a man who knew his duty and did it.[2]

Armed with these amulets, I made up my little mind to seek my fortune. When I had found it, I thought I would drive home in a coach and six, and claim my bride. I cried a little more at the idea of such a triumph, but soon dried my eyes and came out of the court to pursue my plans. These were, first to go (as a species of investment) and see the giants in Guildhall, out of whom I felt it not improbable that some prosperous adventure would arise; failing that contingency, to try about the city for any opening of a Whittington nature; baffled in that too, to go into the army as a drummer.

So, I began to ask my way to Guildhall: which I thought meant, somehow, Gold or Golden Hall; I was too knowing to ask my way to the giants, for I felt it would make people laugh. I remember how immensely broad the streets seemed now I was alone, how high the houses, how grand and mysterious everything. When I came to Temple Bar, it took me half-an-hour to stare at it, and I left it unfinished even then. I had read about heads being exposed on the top of Temple Bar, and it seemed a wicked old place, albeit a noble monument of architecture and a paragon of utility. When at last I got away from it, behold, I came, the next minute, on the figures at St Dunstan's! Who could see those obliging monsters strike upon the bells and go? Between the quarters there was the toyshop to look at – still there, at this present writing, in a new form – and even when that enchanted spot was escaped from, after an hour and more, then St Paul's arose, and how was I to get beyond its dome, or to take my eyes from its cross of gold? I found it a long journey to the giants, and a slow one.

I came into their presence at last, and gazed up at them with dread and veneration. They looked better-tempered, and were altogether more shiny-faced, than I had expected; but they were very big, and, as I judged their pedestals to be about forty feet high, I considered that they would be very big indeed if they were walking on the stone pavement. I was in a state of mind as to these and all such figures, which I suppose holds equally with most children. While I knew them to be images made of something that was not flesh and blood, I still invested them with attributes of life – with consciousness of my being there, for example, and the power of keeping a sly eye upon me. Being very tired I got into the corner under Magog, to be out of the way of his eye, and fell asleep.

When I started up after a long nap, I thought the giants were roaring, but it was only the city. The place was just the same as when I fell asleep: no beanstalk, no fairy, no princess, no dragon, no opening in life of any kind. So, being hungry, I thought I would buy something to eat, and bring it in there and eat it, before going forth to seek my fortune on the Whittington plan.

I was not ashamed of buying a penny roll in a baker's shop, but I looked into a number of cooks' shops before I could muster courage to go into one. At last I saw a pile of cooked sausages in a window with the label, 'Small Germans, A Penny.' Emboldened by knowing what to ask for, I went in and said, 'If you please will you sell me a small German?' which they did, and I took it, wrapped in paper in my pocket, to Guildhall.

The giants were still lying by, in their sly way, pretending to take no notice, so I sat down in another corner, when what should I see before me but a dog with his ears cocked. He was a black dog, with a bit of white over one eye, and bits of white and tan in his paws, and he wanted to play – frisking about me, rubbing his nose against me, dodging at me sideways, shaking his head and pretending to run away backwards, and making himself good-naturedly ridiculous, as if he had no consideration for himself, but wanted to raise my spirits. Now, when I saw this dog I thought of Whittington, and felt that things were coming right; I encouraged him by saying, 'Hi, boy! Poor fellow! Good dog!' and was satisfied that he was to be my dog for ever afterwards, and that he would help me to seek my fortune.

Very much comforted by this (I had cried a little at odd times ever since I was lost), I took the small German out of my pocket, and began my dinner by biting off a bit and throwing it to the dog, who immediately swallowed it with a one-sided jerk, like a pill. While I took a bit myself, and he looked me in the face for a second piece, I considered by what name I should call him. I thought Merrychance would be an expressive name, under the circumstances; and I was elated, I recollect, by inventing such a good one, when Merrychance began to growl at me in a most ferocious manner.

I wondered he was not ashamed of himself, but he didn't care for that; on the contrary he growled a good deal more. With his mouth watering, and his eyes glistening, and his nose in a very damp state, and his head very much on one side, he sidled about on the pavement in a threatening manner and growled at me, until he suddenly made a snap at the small German, tore it out of my hand, and went off with it. He never came back to help me seek my fortune. From that hour to the present, when I am forty years of age, I have never seen my faithful Merrychance again.

I felt very lonely. Not so much for the loss of the small German, though it was delicious (I knew nothing about highly peppered horse at that time), as on account of Merrychance's disappointing me so cruelly; for I had hoped he would do every friendly thing but speak, and perhaps even come to that. I cried a little more, and began to wish that the object of my affections had been lost with me, for company's sake. But, then I remembered that *she* could not go into the army as a drummer; and I dried my eyes and ate my loaf. Coming out, I met a milk-woman, of whom I bought a pennyworth of milk; quite set up again by my repast, I began to roam about the city, and to seek my fortune in the Whittington direction.

When I go into the city, now, it makes me sorrowful to think that I am quite an artful wretch. Strolling about it as a lost child, I thought of the British Merchant and the Lord Mayor, and was full of reverence. Strolling about it now, I laugh at the sacred liveries of state, and get indignant with the corporation as one of the strongest practical jokes of the present day. What did I know then, about the multitude who are always being disappointed in the city; who are always expecting to meet a party there, and to receive money there, and whose expectations are never fulfilled? What did I know then, about that wonderful person, the friend in the city, who is to do so many things for so many people; who is to get this one into a post at home, and that one into a post abroad; who is to settle with this man's creditors, provide for that man's son, and see that other man paid; who is to 'throw himself' into this grand joint-stock certainty, and is to put his name down on that life assurance directory, and never does anything predicted of him? What did I know, then, about him as the friend of gentle men, Mosaic Arabs and others, usually to be seen at races, and chiefly residing in the neighbourhood of Red Lion Square; and as being unable to discount the whole amount of that paper in money, but as happening to have by him a cask of remarkable fine sherry, a dressing-case, and a Venus by Titian, with which he would be willing to make up the balance? Had I ever heard of him, in those innocent days, as confiding information (which never by any chance turned out to be in the remotest degree correct) to solemn bald men, who mysteriously imparted it to breathless dinner tables? No. Had I ever learned to dread him as a shark, disregard him as a humbug, and know him for a myth? Not I. Had I ever heard of him as associated with tightness in the money market, gloom in consols, the exportation of gold, or that rock ahead in everybody's course, the bushel of wheat? Never. Had I the least idea what was meant by such terms as jobbery, rigging the market, cooking accounts, getting up a dividend, making things pleasant, and the like? Not the slightest. Should I have detected in Mr Hudson[3] himself, a staring carcase of golden veal? By no manner of means. The city was to me a vast emporium of precious stones and metals, casks and bales, honour and generosity, foreign fruits and spices. Every merchant and banker was a compound of Mr Fitz-Warren[4] and Sinbad the Sailor. Smith, Payne, and Smith, when the wind was fair for Barbary and the captain present, were in the habit of calling their servants together (the cross cook included) and asking them to produce their little shipments. Glyn and Halifax had personally undergone great hardships in the valley of diamonds. Baring Brothers had seen Rocs' eggs and travelled with caravans. Rothschild had sat in the Bazaar at Bagdad with rich stuffs for sale; and a veiled lady from the Sultan's harem, riding on a donkey, had fallen in love with him.

Thus I wandered about the city, like a child in a dream, staring at the British merchants, and inspired by a mighty faith in the marvellousness of everything. Up courts and down courts – in and out of yards and little squares – peeping into counting-house passages and running away – poorly feeding the echoes in the court of the South Sea House with my timid steps – roaming down into Austin Friars, and wondering how the Friars used to like it – ever staring at the British merchants, and never tired of the shops – I rambled on, all through the day. In such stories as I made, to account for the different places, I believed as devoutly as in the city itself. I particularly remember that when I found myself on 'change, and saw the shabby people sitting under the placards about ships, I settled that they were misers, who had embarked all their wealth to go and buy gold-dust or something of that sort, and were waiting for their respective captains to come and tell them that they were ready to set sail. I observed that they all munched dry biscuits, and I thought it was to keep off sea-sickness.

This was very delightful; but it still produced no result according to the Whittington precedent. There was a dinner preparing at the Mansion House, and when I peeped in at a grated kitchen window, and saw the men cooks at work in their white caps, my heart began to beat with hope that the Lord Mayor, or the Lady Mayoress, or one of the young princesses their daughters, would look out of an upper apartment and direct me to be taken in. But, nothing of the kind occurred. It was not until I had been peeping in some time that one of the cooks called to me (the window was open), 'Cut away, you sir!' which frightened me so, on account of his black whiskers, that I instantly obeyed.

After that, I came to the India House, and asked a boy what it was, who made faces and pulled my hair before he told me, and behaved altogether in an ungenteel and discourteous manner. Sir James Hogg[5] himself might have been satisfied with the veneration in which I held the India House. I had no doubt of its being the most wonderful, the most magnanimous, the most incorruptible, the most practically disinterested, the most in all respects astonishing, establishment on the face of the earth. I understood the nature of an oath, and would have sworn it to be one entire and perfect chrysolite.

Thinking much about boys who went to India, and who immediately, without being sick, smoked pipes like curled-up bell-ropes, terminating in a large cut-glass sugar basin upside down, I got among the outfitting shops. There, I read the lists of things that were necessary for an India-going boy, and when I came to 'one brace of pistols', thought what happiness to be reserved for such a fate! Still no British merchant seemed at all disposed to take me into his house. The only exception was a chimney-sweep – he looked at me as if he thought me suitable to his business; but I ran away from him.

I suffered very much, all day, from boys; they chased me down turnings, brought me to bay in doorways, and treated me quite savagely, though I am sure I gave them no offence. One boy, who had a stump of black-lead pencil in his pocket, wrote his mother's name and address (as he said) on my white hat, outside the crown. Mrs Blores, Wooden Leg Walk, Tobacco-Stopper Row, Wapping. And I couldn't rub it out.

I recollect resting in a little churchyard after this persecution, disposed to think upon the whole, that if I and the object of my affections could be buried there together, at once, it would be comfortable. But, another nap, and a pump, and a bun, and above all a picture that I saw, brought me round again.

I must have strayed by that time, as I recall my course, into Goodman's Fields, or somewhere thereabouts. The picture represented a scene in a play then performing at a theatre in that neighbourhood which is no longer in existence. It stimulated me to go to that theatre and see that play. I resolved, as there seemed to be nothing doing in the Whittington way, that on the conclusion of the entertainments I would ask my way to the barracks, knock at the gate, and tell them that I understood they were in want of drummers, and there I was. I think I must have been told, but I know I believed, that a soldier was always on duty, day and night, behind every barrack-gate, with a shilling; and that a boy who could by any means be prevailed on to accept it, instantly became a drummer, unless his father paid four hundred pounds.

I found out the theatre – of its external appearance I only remember the loyal initials G.R. untidily painted in yellow ochre on the front – and waited, with a pretty large crowd, for the opening of the gallery doors. The greater part of the sailors and others composing the crowd, were of the lowest description, and their conversation was not improving; but I understood little or nothing of what was bad in it then, and it had no depraving influence on me. I have wondered since, how long it would take, by means of such association, to corrupt a child nurtured as I had been, and innocent as I was.

Whenever I saw that my appearance attracted attention, either outside the doors or afterwards within the theatre, I pretended to look out for somebody who was taking care of me, and from whom I was separated, and to exchange nods and smiles with that creature of my imagination. This answered very well. I had my sixpence clutched in my hand ready to pay; and when the doors opened, with a clattering of bolts, and some screaming from women in the crowd, I went on with the current like a straw. My sixpence was rapidly swallowed up in the money-taker's pigeon-hole, which looked to me like a sort of mouth, and I got into the freer staircase above and ran on (as everybody else did) to get a good place. When I came to the back of the gallery, there were very few people in it, and the seats looked so horribly steep, and so like a diving arrangement to send me, headforemost, into the pit, that I held by one of them in a terrible fright. However, there was a good-natured baker with a young woman, who gave me his hand, and we all three scrambled over the seats together down into the corner of the first row. The baker was very fond of the young woman, and kissed her a good deal in the course of the evening.

I was no sooner comfortably settled, than a weight fell upon my mind, which tormented it most dreadfully, and which I must explain. It was a benefit night – the benefit of the comic actor – a little fat man with a very large face and, as I thought then, the smallest and most diverting hat that ever was seen. This comedian, for the gratification of his friends and patrons, had undertaken to sing a comic song on a donkey's back, and afterwards to give away the donkey so distinguished, by lottery. In this lottery, every person admitted to the pit and gallery had a chance. On paying my six pence, I had received the number forty-seven; and I now thought, in a perspiration of terror, what should I ever do if that number was to come up the prize, and I was to win the donkey!

It made me tremble all over to think of the possibility of my good fortune. I knew I never could conceal the fact of my holding forty-seven, in case that number came up, because, not to speak of my confusion, which would immediately condemn me, I had shown my number to the baker. Then, I pictured to myself the being called upon to come down on the stage and receive the donkey. I thought how all the people would shriek when they saw it had fallen to a little fellow like me. How should I lead him out – for of course he wouldn't go? If he began to bray, what should I do? If he kicked, what would become of me? Suppose he backed into the stage-door, and stuck there, with me upon him? For I felt that if I won him, the comic actor would have me on his back, the moment he could touch me. Then if I got him out of the theatre, what was I to do with him? How was I to feed him? Where was I to stable him? It was bad enough to have gone astray by myself, but to go astray with a donkey, too, was a calamity more tremendous than I could bear to contemplate.

These apprehensions took away all my pleasure in the first piece. When the ship came on – a real man-of-war she was called in the bills – and rolled prodigiously in a very heavy sea, I couldn't, even in the terrors of the storm, forget the donkey. It was awful to see the sailors pitching about, with telescopes and speaking trumpets (they looked very tall indeed aboard the man-of-war), and it was awful to suspect the pilot of treachery, though impossible to avoid it, for when he cried – 'We are lost! To the raft, to the raft! A thunderbolt has struck the main-mast!' – I myself saw him take the main-mast out of its socket and drop it overboard; but even these impressive circumstances paled before my dread of the donkey. Even when the good sailor (and he was very good) came to good fortune, and the bad sailor (and he was very bad) threw himself into the ocean from the summit of a curious rock, presenting something of the appearance of a pair of steps, I saw the dreadful donkey through my tears.

At last the time came when the fiddlers struck up the comic song, and the dreaded animal, with new shoes on, as I inferred from the noise they made, came clattering in with the comic actor on his back. He was dressed out with ribbons (I mean the donkey was) and as he persisted in turning his tail to the audience, the comedian got off him, turned about, and sitting with his face that way, sang the song three times, amid thunders of applause. All this time, I was fearfully agitated; and when two pale people, a good deal splashed with the mud of the streets, were invited out of the pit to superintend the drawing of the lottery, and were received with a round of laughter from everybody else, I could have begged and prayed them to have mercy on me, and not draw number forty-seven.

But, I was soon put out of my pain now, for a gentleman behind me, in a flannel jacket and a yellow neckerchief, who had eaten two fried soles and all his pockets-full of nuts before the storm began to rage, answered to the winning number, and went down to take possession of the prize. This gentleman had appeared to know the donkey, rather, from the moment of his entrance, and had taken a great interest in his proceedings; driving him to himself, if I use an intelligible phrase, and saying, almost in my ear, when he made any mistake, 'Kum up, you precious Moke. Kum up!' He was thrown by the donkey on first mounting him, to the great delight of the audience (including myself), but rode him off with great skill afterwards, and soon returned to his seat quite calm. Calmed myself by the immense relief I had sustained, I enjoyed the rest of the performance very much indeed. I remember there were a good many dances, some in fetters and some in roses, and one by a most divine little creature, who made the object of my affections look but commonplace. In the concluding drama, she reappeared as a boy (in arms, mostly), and was fought for, several times. I rather think a baron wanted to drown her, and was on various occasions prevented by the comedian, a ghost, a Newfoundland dog, and a church bell. I only remember beyond this, that I wondered where the Baron expected to go to, and that he went there in a shower of sparks. The lights were turned out while the sparks died out, and it appeared to me as if the whole play – ship, donkey, men and women, divine little creature, and all – were a wonderful firework that had gone off, and left nothing but dust and darkness behind it.

It was late when I got out into the streets, and there was no moon, and there were no stars, and the rain fell heavily. When I emerged from the dispersing crowd, the ghost and the Baron had an ugly look in my remembrance; I felt unspeakably forlorn; and now, for the first time, my little bed and the dear familiar faces came before me, and touched my heart. By daylight, I had never thought of the grief at home. I had never thought of my mother. I had never thought of anything but adapting myself to the circumstances in which I found myself, and going to seek my fortune.

For a boy who could do nothing but cry, and run about, saying 'O I am lost!' to think of going into the army was, I felt sensible, out of the question. I abandoned the idea of asking my way to the barracks – or rather the idea abandoned me – and ran about, until I found a watchman in his box. It is amazing to me, now, that he should have been sober; but I am inclined to think he was too feeble to get drunk.

This venerable man took me to the nearest watch-house; I say he took me, but in fact I took him, for when I think of us in the rain, I recollect that we must have made a composition, like a vignette of Infancy leading Age. He had a dreadful cough, and was obliged to lean against a wall, whenever it came on. We got at last to the watch-house, a warm and drowsy sort of place embellished with great-coats and rattles hanging up. When a paralytic messenger had been sent to make inquiries about me, I fell asleep by the fire, and awoke no more until my eyes opened on my father's face. This is literally and exactly how I went astray. They used to say I was an odd child, and I suppose I was. I am an odd man perhaps.

Shade of Somebody, forgive me for the disquiet I must have caused thee! When I stand beneath the Lion, even now, I see thee rushing up and down, refusing to be comforted. I have gone astray since, many times, and farther afield. May I therein have given less disquiet to others, than herein I gave to thee!

Scotland Yard

Scotland Yard is a small – a very small – tract of land, bounded on one side by the river Thames, on the other by the gardens of Northumberland House: abutting at one end on the bottom of Northumberland Street, at the other on the back of Whitehall Place. When this territory was first accidentally discovered by a country gentleman who lost his way in the Strand, some years ago, the original settlers were found to be a tailor, a publican, two eating-house keepers, and a fruit-pie maker; and it was also found to contain a race of strong and bulky men, who repaired to the wharfs in Scotland Yard regularly every morning about five or six o'clock, to fill heavy wagons with coal, with which they proceeded to distant places up the country, and supplied the inhabitants with fuel. When they had emptied their wagons, they again returned for a fresh supply; and this trade was continued throughout the year.

As the settlers derived their subsistence from ministering to the wants of these primitive traders, the articles exposed for sale, and the places where they were sold, bore strong outward marks of being expressly adapted to their tastes and wishes. The tailor displayed in his window a Lilliputian pair of leather gaiters, and a diminutive round frock, while each doorpost was appropriately garnished with a model of a coal sack. The two eating-house keepers exhibited joints of a magnitude, and puddings of a solidity, which coal-heavers alone could appreciate; and the fruit-pie maker displayed on his well-scrubbed window-board large white compositions of flour and dripping ornamented with pink stains, giving rich promise of the fruit within, which made their huge mouths water, as they lingered past.

But the choicest spot in all Scotland Yard was the old public house in the corner. Here, in a dark wainscoted room of ancient appearance, cheered by the glow of a mighty fire, and decorated with an enormous clock, whereof the face was white, and the figures black, sat the lusty coal-heavers, quaffing large draughts of Barclay's best, and puffing forth volumes of smoke, which wreathed heavily above their heads, and involved the room in a thick dark cloud. From this apartment might their voices be heard on a winter's night, penetrating to the very bank of the river, as they shouted out some sturdy chorus, or roared forth the burden of a popular song; dwelling upon the last few words with a strength and length of emphasis which made the very roof tremble above them.

Here, too, would they tell old legends of what the Thames was in ancient times, when the Patent Shot Manufactory[6] wasn't built, and Waterloo Bridge had never been thought of; and then they would shake their heads with portentous looks, to the deep edification of the rising generation of heavers, who crowded round them, and wondered where all this would end; whereat the tailor would take his pipe solemnly from his mouth, and say how that he hoped it might end well, but he very much doubted whether it would or not, and couldn't rightly tell what to make of it – a mysterious expression of opinion, delivered with a semi-prophetic air, which never failed to elicit the fullest concurrence of the assembled company; and so they would go on drinking and wondering till ten o'clock came, and with it the tailor's wife to fetch him home, when the little party broke up, to meet again in the same room, and say and do precisely the same things, on the following evening at the same hour.

About this time the barges that came up the river began to bring vague rumours to Scotland Yard of somebody in the city having been heard to say, that the Lord Mayor had threatened in so many words to pull down the old London bridge, and build up a new one. At first these rumours were disregarded as idle tales, wholly destitute of foundation, for nobody in Scotland Yard doubted that if the Lord Mayor contemplated any such dark design, he would just be clapped up in the Tower for a week or two, and then killed off for high treason.

By degrees, however, the reports grew stronger, and more frequent, and at last a barge, laden with numerous chaldrons of the best Wallsend,[7] brought up the positive intelligence that several of the arches of the old bridge were stopped, and that preparations were actually in progress for constructing the new one. What an excitement was visible in the old taproom on that memorable night! Each man looked into his neighbour's face, pale with alarm and astonishment, and read therein an echo of the sentiments which filled his own breast. The oldest heaver present proved to demonstration, that the moment the piers were removed, all the water in the Thames would run clean off, and leave a dry gully in its place. What was to become of the coal-barges – of the trade of Scotland Yard – of the very existence of its population? The tailor shook his head more sagely than usual, and grimly pointing to a knife on the table, bid them wait and see what happened. He said nothing – not he; but if the Lord Mayor didn't fall a victim to popular indignation, why he would be rather astonished; that was all.

They did wait; barge after barge arrived, and still no tidings of the assassination of the Lord Mayor. The first stone was laid: it was done by a Duke – the King's brother. Years passed away, and the bridge was opened by the King himself. In course of time, the piers were removed; and when the people in Scotland Yard got up next morning in the confident expectation of being able to step over to Pedlar's Acre without wetting the soles of their shoes, they found to their unspeakable astonishment that the water was just where it used to be!

A result so different from that which they had anticipated from this first improvement, produced its full effect upon the inhabitants of Scotland Yard. One of the eating-house keepers began to court public opinion, and to look for customers among a new class of people. He covered his little dining tables with white cloths, and got a painter's apprentice to inscribe something about hot joints from twelve till two, in one of the little panes of his shop window. Improvement began to march with rapid strides to the very threshold of Scotland Yard. A new market sprung up at Hungerford, and the police commissioners established their office in Whitehall Place. The traffic in Scotland Yard increased; fresh members were added to the House of Commons, the metropolitan representatives found it a near cut, and many other foot passengers followed their example.

We marked the advance of civilisation, and beheld it with a sigh. The eating-house keeper who manfully resisted the innovation of tablecloths, was losing ground every day, as his opponent gained it, and a deadly feud sprung up between them. The genteel one no longer took his evening's pint in Scotland Yard, but drank gin and water at a 'parlour' in Parliament Street. The fruit-pie maker still continued to visit the old room, but he took to smoking cigars, and began to call himself a pastry-cook, and to read the papers. The old heavers still assembled round the ancient fireplace, but their talk was mournful: and the loud song and the joyous shout were heard no more.

And what is Scotland Yard now? How have its old customs changed; and how has the ancient simplicity of its inhabitants faded away! The old tottering public house is converted into a spacious and lofty 'wine vault'; gold leaf has been used in the construction of the letters which emblazon its exterior, and the poet's art has been called into requisition, to intimate that if you drink a certain description of ale, you must hold fast by the rail. The tailor exhibits in his window the pattern of a foreign-looking brown surtout, with silk buttons, a fur collar, and fur cuffs. He wears a stripe down the outside of each leg of his trousers: and we have detected his assistants (for he has assistants now) in the act of sitting on the shop-board in the same uniform.

At the other end of the little row of houses a boot-maker has established himself in a brick box, with the additional innovation of a first floor; and here he exposes for sale, boots – real Wellington boots – an article which a few years ago, none of the original inhabitants had ever seen or heard of. It was but the other day, that a dressmaker opened another little box in the middle of the row; and, when we thought that the spirit of change could produce no alteration beyond that, a jeweller appeared, and not content with exposing gilt rings and copper bracelets out of number, put up an announcement, which still sticks in his window, that ladies' ears may be pierced within. The dressmaker employs a young lady who wears pockets in her apron; and the tailor informs the public that gentlemen may have their own materials made up.

Amidst all this change, and restlessness, and innovation, there remains but one old man, who seems to mourn the downfall of this ancient place. He holds no converse with human kind, but, seated on a wooden bench at the angle of the wall which fronts the crossing from Whitehall Place, watches in silence the gambols of his sleek and well-fed dogs. He is the presiding genius of Scotland Yard. Years and years have rolled over his head; but, in fine weather or in foul, hot or cold, wet or dry, hail, rain, or snow, he is still in his accustomed spot. Misery and want are depicted in his countenance; his form is bent by age, his head is grey with length of trial, but there he sits from day to day, brooding over the past; and thither he will continue to drag his feeble limbs, until his eyes have closed upon Scotland Yard, and upon the world together.

A few years hence, and the antiquarian of another generation, looking into some mouldy record of the strife and passions that agitated the world in these times, may glance his eye over the pages we have just filled: and on all his knowledge of the history of the past, not all his black-letter lore, or his skill in book-collecting, not all the dry studies of a long life, or the dusty volumes that have cost him a fortune, may help him to the whereabouts, either of Scotland Yard, or of any one of the landmarks we have mentioned in describing it.

Seven Dials

We have always been of opinion that if Tom King and the Frenchman[8] had not immortalised Seven Dials, Seven Dials would have immortalised itself. Seven Dials! the region of song and poetry – first effusions, and last dying speeches: hallowed by the names of Catnach and of Pitts[9] – names that will entwine themselves with costermongers, and barrel organs, when penny magazines shall have superseded penny yards of song, and capital punishment be unknown!

Look at the construction of the place. The Gordian knot was all very well in its way: so was the maze of Hampton Court: so is the maze at the Beulah Spa: so were the ties of stiff white neckcloths, when the difficulty of getting one on, was only to be equalled by the apparent impossibility of ever getting it off again. But what involutions can compare with those of Seven Dials – where is there such another maze of streets, courts, lanes, and alleys – where such a pure mixture of Englishmen and Irishmen, as in this complicated part of London? We boldly aver that we doubt the veracity of the legend to which we have adverted. We *can* suppose a man rash enough to inquire at random – at a house with lodgers too – for a Mr Thompson, with all but the certainty before his eyes, of finding at least two or three Thompsons in any house of moderate dimensions; but a Frenchman – a Frenchman – in Seven Dials! Pooh! He was an Irishman. Tom King's education had been neglected in his infancy, and as he couldn't understand half the man said, he took it for granted he was talking French.

The stranger who finds himself in 'The Dials' for the first time, and stands Belzoni-like,[10] at the entrance of seven obscure passages, uncertain which to take, will see enough around him to keep his curiosity and attention awake for no inconsiderable time. From the irregular square into which he has plunged, the streets and courts dart in all directions, until they are lost in the unwholesome vapour which hangs over the house-tops, and renders the dirty perspective uncertain and confined; and lounging at every corner, as if they came there to take a few gasps of such fresh air as has found its way so far, but is too much exhausted already, to be enabled to force itself into the narrow alleys around, are groups of people, whose appearance and dwellings would fill any mind but a regular Londoner's with astonishment.

On one side, a little crowd has collected round a couple of ladies, who having imbibed the contents of various 'three-outs' of gin and bitters in the course of the morning, have at length differed on some point of domestic arrangement, and are on the eve of settling the quarrel satisfactorily, by an appeal to blows, greatly to the interest of other ladies who live in the same house, and tenements adjoining, and who are all partisans on one side or other.

'Vy don't you pitch into her, Sarah?' exclaims one half-dressed matron, by way of encouragement. 'Vy don't you? if *my* 'usband had treated her with a drain last night, unbeknown to me, I'd tear her precious eyes out – a wixen!'

'What's the matter, ma'am?' inquires another old woman, who has just bustled up to the spot.

'Matter!' replies the first speaker, talking *at* the obnoxious combatant, 'matter! Here's poor dear Mrs Sulliwin, as has five blessed children of her own, can't go out a charing for one arternoon, but what hussies must be a comin', and 'ticing avay her oun' 'usband, as she's been married to twelve year come next Easter Monday, for I see the certificate ven I vas a drinkin' a cup o' tea vith her, only the wery last blessed Ven'sday as ever vos sent. I 'appen'd to say promiscuously, "Mrs Sulliwin," says I – '

'What do you mean by hussies?' interrupts a champion of the other party, who has evinced a strong inclination throughout to get up a branch fight on her own account ('Hooroa,' ejaculates a potboy in parenthesis, 'put the kye-bosh on her, Mary!'), 'What do you mean by hussies?' reiterates the champion.

'Niver mind,' replies the opposition expressively, 'niver mind; *you* go home, and, ven you're quite sober, mend your stockings.'

This somewhat personal allusion, not only to the lady's habits of intemperance, but also to the state of her wardrobe, rouses her utmost ire, and she accordingly complies with the urgent request of the bystanders to 'pitch in', with considerable alacrity. The scuffle became general, and terminates, in minor play-bill phraseology, with 'arrival of the policemen – interior of the station-house – and impressive *denouement.*'

In addition to the numerous groups who are idling about the gin shops and squabbling in the centre of the road, every post in the open space has its occupant, who leans against it for hours, with listless perseverance. It is odd enough, that one class of men in London, appear to have no enjoyment beyond leaning against posts. We never saw a regular bricklayer's labourer take any other recreation – fighting excepted. Pass through St Giles' in the evening of a week-day – there they are in their fustian dresses, spotted with brick-dust and whitewash – leaning against posts. Walk through Seven Dials on Sunday morning: there they are again – drab or light corduroy trousers, blucher boots, blue coats, and great yellow waistcoats – leaning against posts. The idea of a man dressing himself in his best clothes, to lean against a post all day!

The peculiar character of these streets, and the close resemblance each one bears to its neighbour, by no means tends to decrease the bewilderment in which the inexperienced wayfarer through 'the Dials' finds himself involved. He traverses streets of dirty, straggling houses, with now and then an unexpected court composed of buildings as ill-proportioned and deformed as the half-naked children that wallow in the kennels. Here and there, a little dark chandler's shop, with a cracked bell hung up behind the door to announce the entrance of a customer, or betray the presence of some young gentleman, in whom a passion for shop tills has developed itself at an early age, others, as if for support, against some handsome lofty building, which usurps the place of a low dingy public house; long rows of broken and patched windows expose plants that may have flourished when 'the Dials' were built, in vessels as dirty as 'the Dials' themselves; and shops for the purchase of rags, bones, old iron, and kitchen-stuff, vie in cleanliness with the bird-fanciers' and rabbit-dealers', which one might fancy so many arks, but for the irresistible conviction that no bird in its proper senses, who was permitted to leave one of them, would ever come back again. Brokers' shops, which would seem to have been established by humane individuals, as refuges for destitute bugs, interspersed with announcements of day-schools, penny theatres, petition-writers, mangles, and music for balls or routs, complete the 'still life' of the subject; and dirty men, filthy women, squalid children, fluttering shuttlecocks, noisy battledores, reeking pipes, bad fruit, more than doubtful oysters, attenuated cats, depressed dogs, and anatomical fowls, are its cheerful accompaniments.

If the external appearance of the houses, or a glance at their inhabitants, present but few attractions, a closer acquaintance with either is little calculated to alter one's first impression. Every room has its separate tenant, and every tenant is, by the same mysterious dispensation which causes a country curate to 'increase and multiply' most marvellously, generally the head of a numerous family.

The man in the shop, perhaps, is in the baked 'jemmy'[11] line, or the firewood and hearthstone line, or any other line which requires a floating capital of eighteen-pence or thereabouts: and he and his family live in the shop, and the small back parlour behind it. Then there is an Irish labourer and *his* family in the back kitchen; and a jobbing man – carpet-beater and so forth – with *his* family in the front one. In the front one-pair, there's another man with another wife and family, and in the back one-pair, there's 'a young 'oman as takes in tambour-work, and dresses quite genteel', who talks a good deal about 'my friend', and can't 'a-bear anything low'. The second floor front, and the rest of the lodgers, are just a second edition of the people below, except a shabby-genteel man in the back attic, who has his half-pint of coffee every morning from the coffee-shop next door but one, which boasts a little front den called a coffee-room, with a fireplace, over which is an inscription, politely requesting that, 'to prevent mistakes', customers will 'please to pay on delivery'. The shabby-genteel man is an object of some mystery, but as he leads a life of seclusion, and never was known to buy anything beyond an occasional pen, except half-pints of coffee, penny loaves, and ha'porths of ink, his fellow-lodgers very naturally suppose him to be an author; and rumours are current in the Dials, that he writes poems – for Mr Warren.[12]

Now anybody who passed through the Dials on a hot summer's evening, and saw the different women of the house gossiping on the steps, would be apt to think that all was harmony among them, and that a more primitive set of people than the native Diallers could not be imagined. Alas! the man in the shop ill treats his family; the carpet-beater extends his professional pursuits to his wife; the one-pair front has an undying feud with the two-pair front, in consequence of the two-pair front persisting in dancing over his (the one-pair front's) head, when he and his family have retired for the night; the two-pair back *will* interfere with the front kitchen's children; the Irishman comes home drunk every other night, and attacks everybody; and the one-pair back screams at everything. Animosities spring up between floor and floor; the very cellar asserts his equality. Mrs A– 'smacks' Mrs B–'s child for 'making faces'. Mrs B– forthwith throws cold water over Mrs A–'s child for 'calling names'. The husbands are embroiled – the quarrel becomes general – an assault is the consequence, and a police officer the result.

Gin-Shops

It is a remarkable circumstance, that different trades appear to partake of the disease to which elephants and dogs are especially liable, and to run stark, staring, raving mad, periodically. The great distinction between the animals and the trades is, that the former run mad with a certain degree of propriety – they are very regular in their irregularities. We know the period at which the emergency will arise, and provide against it accordingly. If an elephant run mad, we are all ready for him – kill or cure – pills or bullets, calomel in conserve of roses, or lead in a musket-barrel. If a dog happen to look unpleasantly warm in the summer months, and to trot about the shady side of the streets with a quarter of a yard of tongue hanging out of his mouth, a thick leather muzzle, which has been previously prepared in compliance with the thoughtful injunctions of the legislature, is instantly clapped over his head, by way of making him cooler, and he either looks remarkably unhappy for the next six weeks, or becomes legally insane, and goes mad, as it were, by Act of Parliament. But these trades are as eccentric as comets; nay, worse, for no one can calculate on the recurrence of the strange appearances which betoken the disease. Moreover, the contagion is general, and the quickness with which it diffuses itself, almost incredible.

We will cite two or three cases in illustration of our meaning. Six or eight years ago, the epidemic began to display itself among the linen-drapers and haberdashers. The primary symptoms were an inordinate love of plate-glass, and a passion for gaslights and gilding. The disease gradually progressed, and at last attained a fearful height. Quiet dusty old shops in different parts of town, were pulled down; spacious premises with stuccoed fronts and gold letters, were erected instead; floors were covered with Turkey carpets; roofs supported by massive pillars; doors knocked into windows; a dozen squares of glass into one;

one shopman into a dozen; and there is no knowing what would have been done, if it had not been fortunately discovered, just in time, that the Commissioners in Bankruptcy were as competent to decide such cases as the Commissioners of Lunacy, and that a little confinement and gentle examination did wonders. The disease abated. It died away. A year or two of comparative tranquillity ensued. Suddenly it burst out again amongst the chemists; the symptoms were the same, with the addition of a strong desire to stick the royal arms over the shop-door, and a great rage for mahogany, varnish, and expensive floor-cloth. Then, the hosiers were infected, and began to pull down their shop-fronts with frantic recklessness. The mania again died away, and the public began to congratulate themselves on its entire disappearance, when it burst forth with tenfold violence among the publicans, and keepers of 'wine vaults'. From that moment it has spread among them with unprecedented rapidity, exhibiting a concatenation of all the previous symptoms; onward it has rushed to every part of town, knocking down all the old public houses, and depositing splendid mansions, stone balustrades, rosewood fittings, immense lamps, and illuminated clocks, at the corner of every street.

The extensive scale on which these places are established, and the ostentatious manner in which the business of even the smallest among them is divided into branches, is amusing. A handsome plate of ground glass in one door directs you 'To the Counting-house'; another to the 'Bottle Department'; a third to the 'Wholesale Department'; a fourth to 'The Wine Promenade'; and so forth, until we are in daily expectation of meeting with a 'Brandy Bell', or a 'Whiskey Entrance'. Then, ingenuity is exhausted in devising attractive titles for the different descriptions of gin; and the dram-drinking portion of the community as they gaze upon the gigantic black and white announcements, which are only to be equalled in size by the figures beneath them, are left in a state of pleasing hesitation between 'The Cream of the Valley', 'The Out and Out', 'The No Mistake',

'The Good for Mixing', 'The real Knock-me-down', 'The celebrated Butter Gin', 'The regular Flare-up', and a dozen other, equally inviting and wholesome liqueurs. Although places of this description are to be met with in every second street, they are invariably numerous and splendid in precise proportion to the dirt and poverty of the surrounding neighbourhood. The gin-shops in and near Drury Lane, Holborn, St Giles', Covent Garden, and Clare Market, are the handsomest in London. There is more of filth and squalid misery near those great thoroughfares than in any part of this mighty city.

We will endeavour to sketch the bar of a large gin-shop, and its ordinary customers, for the edification of such of our readers as may not have had opportunities of observing such scenes; and on the chance of finding one well suited to our purpose, we will make for Drury Lane, through the narrow streets and dirty courts which divide it from Oxford Street, and that classical spot adjoining the brewery at the bottom of Tottenham Court Road, best known to the initiated as the 'Rookery'.

The filthy and miserable appearance of this part of London can hardly be imagined by those (and there are many such) who have not witnessed it. Wretched houses with broken windows patched with rags and paper: every room let out to a different family, and in many instances to two or even three – fruit and 'sweet-stuff' manufacturers in the cellars, barbers and red-herring vendors in the front parlours, cobblers in the back; a bird-fancier in the first floor, three families on the second, starvation in the attics, Irishmen in the passage, a 'musician' in the front kitchen, and a charwoman and five hungry children in the back one – filth everywhere – a gutter before the houses and a drain behind – clothes drying and slops emptying, from the windows; girls of fourteen or fifteen, with matted hair, walking about barefoot, and in white great-coats, almost their only covering; boys of all ages, in coats of all sizes and no coats at all; men and women, in every variety of scanty and dirty apparel, lounging, scolding, drinking, smoking, squabbling, fighting, and swearing.

You turn the corner. What a change! All is light and brilliancy. The hum of many voices issues from that splendid gin-shop which forms the commencement of the two streets opposite; and the gay building with the fantastically ornamented parapet, the illuminated clock, the plate-glass windows surrounded by stucco rosettes, and its profusion of gas-lights in richly gilt burners, is perfectly dazzling when contrasted with the darkness and dirt we have just left. The interior is even gayer than the exterior. A bar of French-polished mahogany, elegantly carved, extends the whole width of the place; and there are two side-aisles of great casks, painted green and gold, enclosed within a light brass rail, and bearing such inscriptions, as 'Old Tom, 549'; 'Young Tom, 360'; 'Samson, 1421' – the figures agreeing, we presume, with 'gallons', understood. Beyond the bar is a lofty and spacious saloon, full of the same enticing vessels, with a gallery running round it, equally well furnished. On the counter, in addition to the usual spirit apparatus, are two or three little baskets of cakes and biscuits, which are carefully secured at top with wickerwork, to prevent their contents being unlawfully abstracted. Behind it, are two showily dressed damsels with large necklaces, dispensing the spirits and 'compounds'. They are assisted by the ostensible proprietor of the concern, a stout, coarse fellow in a fur cap, put on very much on one side to give him a knowing air, and to display his sandy whiskers to the best advantage.

The two old washerwomen, who are seated on the little bench to the left of the bar, are rather overcome by the head-dresses and haughty demeanour of the young ladies who officiate. They receive their half-quartern of gin and peppermint, with consider-able deference, prefacing a request for 'one of them soft biscuits' with a 'Jist be good enough, ma'am.' They are quite astonished at the impudent air of the young fellow in a brown coat and bright buttons, who, ushering in his two companions, and walk-ing up to the bar in as careless a manner as if he had been used to green and gold ornaments all his life, winks at one of the young ladies with singular coolness, and calls for a 'kervorten and a three-out-glass', just as if the place were his own. 'Gin for you, sir?' says the young lady when she has drawn it: carefully looking every way but the right one, to show that the wink had no effect upon her. 'For me, Mary, my dear,' replies the gentleman in brown. 'My name ain't Mary as it happens,' says the young girl, rather relaxing as she delivers the change. 'Well, if it ain't, it ought to be,' responds the irresistible one; 'all the Marys as ever I see, was handsome gals.' Here the young lady, not precisely remembering how blushes are managed in such cases, abruptly ends the flirtation by addressing the female in the faded feathers who has just entered, and who, after stating explicitly, to prevent any subsequent misunderstanding, that 'this gentleman pays', calls for 'a glass of port wine and a bit of sugar'.

Those two old men who came in 'just to have a drain' finished their third quartern a few seconds ago; they have made themselves crying drunk; and the fat comfortable-looking elderly women, who had 'a glass of rum-srub' each, having chimed in with their complaints on the hardness of the times, one of the women has agreed to stand a glass round, jocularly observing that 'grief never mended no broken bones, and as good people's wery scarce, what I says is, make the most on 'em, and that's all about it!', a sentiment which appears to afford unlimited satisfaction to those who have nothing to pay.

It is growing late, and the throng of men, women, and children, who have been constantly going in and out, dwindles down to two or three occasional stragglers – cold, wretched-looking creatures, in the last stage of emaciation and disease. The knot of Irish labourers at the lower end of the place, who have been alternately shaking hands with, and threatening the life of each other, for the last hour, become furious in their disputes, and finding it impossible to silence one man, who is particularly anxious to adjust the difference, they resort to the expedient of knocking him down and jumping on him afterwards. The man in the fur cap, and the potboy rush out; a scene of riot and confusion ensues; half the Irishmen get shut out, and the other half get shut in; the potboy is knocked among the tubs in no time; the landlord hits everybody, and everybody hits the landlord; the barmaids scream; the police come in; the rest is a confused mixture of arms, legs, staves, torn coats, shouting, and struggling. Some of the party are borne off to the station-house, and the remainder slink home to beat their wives for complaining, and kick the children for daring to be hungry.

We have sketched this subject very slightly, not only because our limits compel us to do so, but because, if it were pursued farther, it would be painful and repulsive. Well-disposed gentlemen, and charitable ladies, would alike turn with coldness and disgust from a description of the drunken besotted men, and wretched broken-down miserable women, who form no inconsiderable portion of the frequenters of these haunts; forgetting, in the pleasant consciousness of their own rectitude, the poverty of the one, and the temptation of the other. Gin-drinking is a great vice in England, but wretchedness and dirt are a greater; and until you improve the homes of the poor, or persuade a half-famished wretch not to seek relief in the temporary oblivion of his own misery, with the pittance which, divided among his family, would furnish a morsel of bread for each, gin-shops will increase in number and splendour. If Temperance Societies would suggest an antidote against hunger, filth, and foul air, or could establish dispensaries for the gratuitous distribution of bottles of Lethe-water,[13] gin-palaces would be numbered among the things that were.

City of the Absent

When I think I deserve particularly well of myself, and have earned the right to enjoy a little treat, I stroll from Covent Garden into the city of London, after business-hours there, on a Saturday, or – better yet – on a Sunday, and roam about its deserted nooks and corners. It is necessary to the full enjoyment of these journeys that they should be made in summer-time, for then the retired spots that I love to haunt, are at their idlest and dullest. A gentle fall of rain is not objectionable, and a warm mist sets off my favourite retreats to decided advantage.

Among these, city churchyards hold a high place. Such strange churchyards hide in the city of London; churchyards sometimes so entirely detached from churches, always so pressed upon by houses; so small, so rank, so silent, so forgotten, except by the few people who ever look down into them from their smoky windows. As I stand peeping in through the iron gates and rails, I can peel the rusty metal off, like bark from an old tree. The illegible tombstones are all lop-sided, the grave-mounds lost their shape in the rains of a hundred years ago, the Lombardy Poplar or Plane-Tree that was once a drysalter's daughter and several common-councilmen, has withered like those worthies, and its departed leaves are dust beneath it. Contagion of slow ruin overhangs the place. The discoloured tiled roofs of the environing buildings stand so awry, that they can hardly be proof against any stress of weather. Old crazy stacks of chimneys seem to look down as they overhang, dubiously calculating how far they will have to fall. In an angle of the walls, what was once the tool-house of the gravedigger rots away, encrusted with toad-stools. Pipes and spouts for carrying off the rain from the encompassing gables, broken or feloniously cut for old lead long ago, now let the rain drip and splash as it list, upon the weedy earth. Sometimes there is a rusty pump somewhere near, and, as I look in at the rails and meditate, I hear it working under an unknown hand with a creaking protest: as though the departed in the churchyard urged, 'Let us lie here in peace; don't suck us up and drink us!'

One of my best beloved churchyards, I call the churchyard of Saint Ghastly Grim; touching what men in general call it, I have no information.[14] It lies at the heart of the city, and the Blackwall Railway shrieks at it daily. It is a small, small church-yard, with a ferocious, strong, spiked iron gate, like a jail. This gate is ornamented with skulls and cross-bones, larger than the life, wrought in stone; but it likewise came into the mind of Saint Ghastly Grim, that to stick iron spikes a-top of the stone skulls, as though they were impaled, would be a pleasant device. Therefore the skulls grin aloft horribly, thrust through and through with iron spears. Hence, there is attraction of repulsion for me in Saint Ghastly Grim, and, having often contemplated it in the daylight and the dark, I once felt drawn towards it in a thunderstorm at midnight. 'Why not?' I said, in self-excuse. 'I have been to see the Coliseum by the light of the moon; is it worse to go to see Saint Ghastly Grim by the light of the light-ning?' I repaired to the Saint in a hackney cab, and found the skulls most effective, having the air of a public execution, and seeming, as the lightning flashed, to wink and grin with the pain of the spikes. Having no other person to whom to impart my satisfaction, I communicated it to the driver. So far from being responsive, he surveyed me – he was naturally a bottled-nosed, red-faced man – with a blanched countenance. And as he drove me back, he ever and again glanced in over his shoulder through the little front window of his carriage, as mistrusting that I was a fare originally from a grave in the churchyard of Saint Ghastly Grim, who might have flitted home again without paying.

Sometimes, the queer hall of some queer company gives upon a churchyard such as this, and, when the livery dine, you may hear them (if you are looking in through the iron rails, which you never are when I am) toasting their own worshipful prosper-ity. Sometimes, a wholesale house of business, requiring much room for stowage, will occupy one or two or even all three sides of the enclosing space, and the backs of bales of goods will lumber up the windows, as if they were holding some crowded trade-meeting of themselves within. Sometimes, the commanding windows are all blank, and show no more sign of life than the graves below not so much, for *they* tell of what once upon a time was life undoubtedly. Such was the surrounding of one city churchyard that I saw last summer, on a Volunteering Saturday evening towards eight of the clock, when with astonishment I beheld an old, old man and an old, old woman in it, making hay. Yes, of all occupations in this world, making hay! It was a very confined patch of churchyard lying between Gracechurch Street and the Tower, capable of yielding, say an apronful of hay. By what means the old, old man and woman had got into it, with an almost toothless haymaking rake, I could not fathom. No open window was within view; no window at all was within view, sufficiently near the ground to have enabled their old legs to descend from it; the rusty churchyard-gate was locked, the mouldy church was locked. Gravely among the graves, they made hay, all alone by themselves. They looked like Time and his wife. There was but the one rake between them, and they both had hold of it in a pastorally loving manner, and there was hay on the old woman's black bonnet, as if the old man had recently been playful. The old man was quite an obsolete old man, in knee-breeches and coarse grey stockings, and the old woman wore mittens like unto his stockings in texture and in colour. They took no heed of me as I looked on, unable to account for them. The old woman was much too bright for a pew-opener, the old man much too meek for a beadle. On an old tombstone in the foreground between me and them, were two cherubim; but for those celestial embellishments being represented as having no possible use for knee-breeches, stockings, or mittens, I should have compared them with the haymakers, and sought a likeness. I coughed and awoke the echoes, but the haymakers never looked at me. They used the rake with a measured action, drawing the scanty crop towards them; and so I was fain to leave them under three yards and a half of darkening sky, gravely making hay among the graves, all alone by themselves. Perhaps they were spectres, and I wanted a medium.

In another city churchyard of similar cramped dimensions, I saw, that selfsame summer, two comfortable charity children. They were making love – tremendous proof of the vigour of that immortal article, for they were in the graceful uniform under which English Charity delights to hide herself – and they were overgrown, and their legs (his legs at least, for I am modestly incompetent to speak of hers) were as much in the wrong as mere passive weakness of character can render legs. O it was a leaden churchyard, but no doubt a golden ground to those young persons! I first saw them on a Saturday evening, and, perceiving from their occupation that Saturday evening was their trysting-time, I returned that evening se'nnight, and renewed the contemplation of them. They came there to shake the bits of matting which were spread in the church aisles, and they afterwards rolled them up, he rolling his end, she rolling hers, until they met, and over the two once divided now united rolls – sweet emblem! – gave and received a chaste salute. It was so refreshing to find one of my faded churchyards blooming into flower thus, that I returned a second time, and a third, and ultimately this befell: they had left the church door open, in their dusting and arranging. Walking in to look at the church, I became aware, by the dim light, of him in the pulpit, of her in the reading-desk, of him looking down, of her looking up, exchanging tender discourse. Immediately both dived, and became as it were nonexistent on this sphere. With an assumption of innocence I turned to leave the sacred edifice, when an obese form stood in the portal, puffily demanding Joseph, or in default of Joseph, Celia. Taking this monster by the sleeve, and luring him forth on pretence of showing him whom he sought, I gave time for the emergence of Joseph and Celia, who presently came towards us in the churchyard, bending under dusty matting, a

picture of thriving and unconscious industry. It would be super-
fluous to hint that I have ever since deemed this the proudest
passage in my life.

But such instances, or any tokens of vitality, are rare indeed
in my city churchyards. A few sparrows occasionally try to raise
a lively chirrup in their solitary tree – perhaps, as taking a different view of worms from that entertained by humanity – but
they are flat and hoarse of voice, like the clerk, the organ, the
bell, the clergyman, and all the rest of the church-works when
they are wound up for Sunday. Caged larks, thrushes, or black-
birds, hanging in neighbouring courts, pour forth their strains
passionately, as scenting the tree, trying to break out, and see
leaves again before they die, but their song is Willow, Willow –
of a churchyard cast. So little light lives inside the churches of
my churchyards, when the two are coexistent, that it is often
only by an accident and after long acquaintance that I discover
their having stained glass in some odd window. The westering
sun slants into the churchyard by some unwonted entry, a few
prismatic tears drop on an old tombstone, and a window that
I thought was only dirty, is for the moment all bejewelled. Then
the light passes and the colours die. Though even then, if there
be room enough for me to fall back so far as that I can gaze up
to the top of the church tower, I see the rusty vane new burnished, and seeming to look out with a joyful flash over the sea of
smoke at the distant shore of country.

Blinking old men who are let out of workhouses by the
hour, have a tendency to sit on bits of coping stone in these
churchyards, leaning with both hands on their sticks and
asthmatically gasping. The more depressed class of beggars too,
bring hither broken meats, and munch. I am on nodding terms
with a meditative turncock[15] who lingers in one of them, and
whom I suspect of a turn for poetry; the rather, as he looks out of
temper when he gives the fireplug a disparaging wrench with
that large tuning-fork of his which would wear out the shoulder
of his coat, but for a precautionary piece of inlaid leather.

Fire-ladders, which I am satisfied nobody knows anything about, and the keys of which were lost in ancient times, moulder away in the larger churchyards, under eaves like wooden eyebrows; and so removed are those corners from the haunts of men and boys, that once on a fifth of November I found a 'Guy' trusted to take care of himself there, while his proprietors had gone to dinner. Of the expression of his face I cannot report, because it was turned to the wall; but his shrugged shoulders and his ten extended fingers, appeared to denote that he had moralised in his little straw chair on the mystery of mortality until he gave it up as a bad job.

You do not come upon these churchyards violently; there are shades of transition in the neighbourhood. An antiquated news shop, or barber's shop, apparently bereft of customers in the earlier days of George the Third, would warn me to look out for one, if any discoveries in this respect were left for me to make. A very quiet court, in combination with an unaccountable dyer's and scourer's, would prepare me for a churchyard. An exceedingly retiring public house, with a bagatelle-board shadily visible in a sawdusty parlour shaped like an omnibus, and with a shelf of punch-bowls in the bar, would apprise me that I stood near consecrated ground. A 'Dairy', exhibiting in its modest window one very little milk-can and three eggs, would suggest to me the certainty of finding the poultry hard by, pecking at my forefathers. I first inferred the vicinity of Saint Ghastly Grim, from a certain air of extra repose and gloom pervading a vast stack of warehouses.

From the hush of these places, it is congenial to pass into the hushed resorts of business. Down the lanes I like to see the carts and wagons huddled together in repose, the cranes idle, and the warehouses shut. Pausing in the alleys behind the closed banks of mighty Lombard Street, it gives one as good as a rich feeling to think of the broad counters with a rim along the edge, made for telling money out on, the scales for weighing precious metals, the ponderous ledgers, and, above all, the bright copper shovels for shovelling gold. When I draw money, it never seems so much money as when it is shovelled at me out of a bright copper shovel. I like to say 'In gold' and to see seven pounds musically pouring out of the shovel, like seventy; the bank appearing to remark to me – I italicise *appearing* – 'if you want more of this yellow earth, we keep it in barrows at your service.' To think of the banker's clerk with his deft finger turning the crisp edges of the hundred-pound notes he has taken in a fat roll out of a drawer, is again to hear the rustling of that delicious south-cash wind. 'How will you have it?' I once heard this usual question asked at a bank counter of an elderly female, habited in mourning and steeped in simplicity, who answered, open-eyed, crook-fingered, laughing with expectation, 'Anyhow!' Calling these things to mind as I stroll among the banks, I wonder whether the other solitary Sunday man I pass, has designs upon the banks. For the interest and mystery of the matter, I almost hope he may have, and that his confederate may be at this moment taking impressions of the keys of the iron closets in wax, and that a delightful robbery may be in course of transaction. About College Hill, Mark Lane, and so on towards the Tower, and Dockward, the deserted wine-merchants' cellars are fine subjects for consideration; but the deserted money-cellars of the bankers, and their plate-cellars, and their jewel-cellars, what subterranean regions of the wonderful lamp[16] are these! And again: possibly some shoeless boy in rags, passed through this street yesterday, for whom it is reserved to be a banker in the fullness of time, and to be surpassing rich. Such reverses have been, since the days of Whittington; and were, long before. I want to know whether the boy has any foreglittering of that glittering fortune now, when he treads these stones, hungry. Much as I also want to know whether the next man to be hanged at Newgate yonder, had any suspicion upon him that he was moving steadily towards that fate, when he talked so much about the last man who paid the same great debt at the same small debtors' door.

Where are all the people who on busy working-days pervade these scenes? The locomotive banker's clerk, who carries a black portfolio chained to him by a chain of steel, where is he? Does he go to bed with his chain on – to church with his chain on – or does he lay it by? And if he lays it by, what becomes of his portfolio when he is unchained for a holiday? The wastepaper baskets of these closed counting-houses would let me into many hints of business matters if I had the exploration of them; and what secrets of the heart should I discover on the 'pads' of the young clerks – the sheets of cartridge-paper and blotting-paper interposed between their writing and their desks! Pads are taken into confidence on the tenderest occasions, and oftentimes when I have made a business visit, and have sent in my name from the outer office, have I had it forced on my discursive notice that the officiating young gentleman has over and over again inscribed AMELIA, in ink of various dates, on corners of his pad. Indeed, the pad may be regarded as the legitimate modern successor of the old forest-tree: whereon these young knights (having no attainable forest nearer than Epping) engrave the names of their mistresses. After all, it is a more satisfactory process than carving, and can be oftener repeated. So these courts in their Sunday rest are courts of love omnipotent (I rejoice to bethink myself), dry as they look. And here is Garraway's,[17] bolted and shuttered hard and fast! It is possible to imagine the man who cuts the sandwiches, on his back in a hayfield; it is possible to imagine his desk, like the desk of a clerk at church, without him; but imagination is unable to pursue the men who wait at Garraway's all the week for the men who never come. When they are forcibly put out of Garraway's on Saturday night – which they must be, for they never would go out of their own accord – where do they vanish until Monday morning? On the first Sunday that I ever strayed here, I expected to find them hovering about these lanes, like restless ghosts, and trying to peep into Garraway's through chinks in the shutters, if not endeavouring to turn the lock of the door with false keys, picks, and screwdrivers. But the wonder is, that they go clean away! And now I think of it, the wonder is, that every working-day pervader of these scenes goes clean away. The man who sells the dogs' collars and the little toy coal-scuttles, feels under as great an obligation to go afar off, as Glyn and Co., or Smith, Payne, and Smith. There is an old monastery-crypt under Garraway's (I have been in it among the port wine), and perhaps Garraway's, taking pity on the mouldy men who wait in its public-room all their lives, gives them cool house-room down there over Sundays; but the catacombs of Paris would not be large enough to hold the rest of the missing. This characteristic of London city greatly helps its being the quaint place it is in the weekly pause of business, and greatly helps my Sunday sensation in it of being the last man. In my solitude, the ticket-porters being all gone with the rest, I venture to breathe to the quiet bricks and stones my confidential wonderment why a ticket-porter, who never does any work with his hands, is bound to wear a white apron, and why a great ecclesiastical dignitary, who never does any work with his hands either, is equally bound to wear a black one.

The Giant Chronicles

Once upon a time, that is to say, in this our time – the exact year, month, and day are of no matter – there dwelt in the city of London a substantial citizen, who united in his single person the dignities of wholesale fruiterer, alderman, common-councilman, and member of the worshipful company of Patten-makers;[18] who had superadded to these extraordinary distinctions the important post and title of sheriff, and who at length, and to crown all, stood next in rotation for the high and honourable office of Lord Mayor.

He was a very substantial citizen indeed. His face was like the full moon in a fog, with two little holes punched out for his eyes, a very ripe pear stuck on for his nose, and a wide gash to serve for a mouth. The girth of his waistcoat was hung up and lettered in his tailor's shop as an extraordinary curiosity. He breathed like a heavy snorer, and his voice in speaking came thickly forth, as if it were oppressed and stifled by featherbeds. He trod the ground like an elephant, and ate and drank like – like nothing but an alderman, as he was.

This worthy citizen had risen to his great eminence from small beginnings. He had once been a very lean, weazen little boy, never dreaming of carrying such a weight of flesh upon his bones or of money in his pockets, and glad enough to take his dinner at a baker's door, and his tea at a pump. But he had long ago forgotten all this, as it was proper that a wholesale fruiterer, alderman, common-councilman, member of the worshipful company of Patten-makers, past sheriff, and, above all, a Lord Mayor that was to be, should; and he never forgot it more completely in all his life than on the eighth of November in the year of his election to the great golden civic chair, which was the day before his grand dinner at Guildhall.

It happened that as he sat that evening all alone in his counting-house, looking over the bill of fare for next day, and checking off the fat capons in fifties and the turtle-soup by the hundred quarts for his private amusement – it happened that, as he sat alone, occupied in these pleasant calculations, a strange man came in and asked him how he did: adding, 'If I am half as much changed as you, sir, you have no recollection of me, I am sure.'

The strange man was not over and above well dressed, and was very far from being fat or rich-looking in any sense of the word, yet he spoke with a kind of modest confidence, and assumed an easy, gentlemanly sort of an air, to which nobody but a rich man can lawfully presume. Besides this, he interrupted the good citizen just as he had reckoned 372 fat capons, and was carrying them over to the next column; and as if that were not aggravation enough, the learned recorder for the city of London had only ten minutes previously gone out at that very same door, and had turned round and said, 'Good night, my lord.' Yes, he had said, 'my lord;' – he, a man of birth and education, of the honourable society of the Middle Temple, barrister at law – he who had an uncle in the House of Commons, and an aunt almost, but not quite, in the House of Lords (for she had married a feeble peer, and made him vote as she liked) – he, this man, this learned recorder, had said, 'my lord.' 'I'll not wait till tomorrow to give you your title, my Lord Mayor,' says he, with a bow and a smile; 'you are Lord Mayor *de facto*, if not *de jure*. Good night, my lord.'

The Lord Mayor elect thought of this, and turning to the stranger, and sternly bidding him 'go out of his private counting-house', brought forward the 372 fat capons, and went on with the account.

'Do you remember,' said the other, stepping forward – '*Do you remember little Joe Toddyhigh?*'

The port wine fled for a moment from the fruiterer's nose as he muttered, 'Joe Toddyhigh! What about Joe Toddyhigh?'

'I am Joe Toddyhigh,' cried the visitor. 'Look at me, look hard at me; harder, harder. You know me now? You know little Joe again? What a happiness to us both to meet the very night before your grandeur! Oh! give me your hand, Jack – both hands – both, for the sake of old times.'

'You pinch me, sir. You're a hurting of me,' said the Lord Mayor elect, pettishly. 'Don't – suppose anybody should come – Mr Toddyhigh, sir.'

'Mr Toddyhigh!' repeated the other, ruefully.

'Oh! don't bother,' said the Lord Mayor elect, scratching his head. 'Dear me! Why, I thought you was dead. What a fellow you are!'

Indeed, it was a pretty state of things, and worthy the tone of vexation and disappointment in which the Lord Mayor spoke. Joe Toddyhigh had been a poor boy with him at Hull, and had oftentimes divided his last penny and parted his last crust to relieve his wants; for though Joe was a destitute child in those times, he was as faithful and affectionate in his friendship as ever man of might could be. They parted one day to seek their fortunes in different directions. Joe went to sea, and the now wealthy citizen begged his way to London. They separated with many tears, like foolish fellows as they were, and agreed to remain fast friends, and if they lived, soon to communicate again.

When he was an errand-boy, and even in the early days of his apprenticeship, the citizen had many a time trudged to the post office to ask if there were any letter from poor little Joe, and had gone home again with tears in his eyes, when he found no news of his only friend. The world is a wide place, and it was a long time before the letter came; when it did, the writer was forgotten. It turned from white to yellow from lying in the post office with nobody to claim it, and, in course of time, was torn up with five hundred others, and sold for waste paper. And now at last, and when it might least have been expected, here was this Joe Toddyhigh turning up and claiming acquaintance with a great public character, who on the morrow would be cracking jokes with the Prime Minister of England, and who had only, at any time during the next twelve months, to say the word, and he could shut up Temple Bar, and make it no thoroughfare for the King himself!

'I am sure I don't know what to say, Mr Toddyhigh,' said the Lord Mayor elect; 'I really don't. It's very inconvenient. I'd sooner have given twenty pound – it's very inconvenient, really.'

A thought had struggled into his mind, that perhaps his old friend might say something passionate, which would give him an excuse for being angry himself. No such thing. Joe looked at him steadily, but very mildly, and did not open his lips.

'Of course I shall pay you what I owe you,' said the Lord Mayor elect, fidgeting in his chair. 'You lent me – I think it was a shilling, or some small coin – when we parted company, and that of course I shall pay, with good interest. I can pay my way with any man, and always have done. If you look into the mansion house the day after tomorrow – some time after dusk – and ask for my private clerk, you'll find he has a draft for you. I haven't got time to say anything more just now, unless' – he hesitated, for, coupled with a strong desire to glitter for once in all his glory in the eyes of his former companion, was a distrust of his appearance, which might be more shabby than he could tell by that feeble light – 'unless you'd like to come to the dinner tomorrow. I don't mind your having this ticket, if you like to take it. A great many people would give their ears for it, I can tell you.'

His old friend took the card without speaking a word, and instantly departed. His sunburnt face and grey hair were present to the citizen's mind for a moment; but by the time he reached 381 fat capons, he had quite forgotten him.

Joe Toddyhigh had never been in the capital of Europe before, and he wandered up and down the streets that night, amazed at the number of churches and other public buildings, the splendour of the shops, the riches that were heaped up on every side, the glare of light in which they were displayed, and the concourse of people who hurried to and fro, indifferent apparently to all the wonders that surrounded them. But in all the long streets and broad squares there were none but strangers; it was quite a relief to turn down a byway and hear his own footsteps on the pavement. He went home to his inn; thought that London was a dreary, desolate place, and felt disposed to doubt the existence of one true-hearted man in the whole worshipful company of Patten-makers. Finally, he went to bed, and dreamed that he and the Lord Mayor elect were boys again.

He went next day to the dinner, and when, in a burst of light and music, and in the midst of splendid decorations and surrounded by brilliant company, his former friend appeared at the head of the hall, and was hailed with shouts and cheering, he cheered and shouted with the best, and for the moment could have cried. The next moment he cursed his weakness in behalf of a man so changed and selfish, and quite hated a jolly-looking old gentleman opposite for declaring himself, in the pride of his heart, a Patten-maker.

As the banquet proceeded, he took more and more to heart the rich citizen's unkindness – and that, not from any envy, but because he felt that a man of his state and fortune could all the better afford to recognise an old friend, even if he were poor and obscure. The more he thought of this, the more lonely and sad he felt. When the company dispersed and adjourned to the ball-room, he paced the hall and passages alone, ruminating in a very melancholy condition upon the disappointment he had experienced.

It chanced, while he was lounging about in this moody state, that he stumbled upon a flight of stairs, dark, steep, and narrow, which he ascended without any thought about the matter, and so came into a little music-gallery, empty and deserted. From this elevated post, which commanded the whole hall, he amused himself in looking down upon the attendants, who were clearing away the fragments of the feast very lazily, and drinking out of all the bottles and glasses with most commendable perseverance.

His attention gradually relaxed, and he fell fast asleep.

When he awoke he thought there must be something the matter with his eyes; but, rubbing them a little, he soon found that the moonlight was really streaming through the east window, that the lamps were all extinguished, and that he was alone. He listened, but no distant murmur in the echoing passages, not even the shutting of a door, broke the deep silence; he groped his way down the stairs, and found that the door at the bottom was locked on the other side. He began now to comprehend that he must have slept a long time, that he had been overlooked, and was shut up there for the night.

His first sensation, perhaps, was not altogether a comfortable one, for it was a dark, chilly, earthy-smelling place, and something too large for a man so situated to feel at home in. However, when the momentary consternation of his surprise was over, he made light of the accident, and resolved to feel his way up the stairs again, and make himself as comfortable as he could in the gallery until morning. As he turned to execute this purpose, he heard the clocks strike three.

Any such invasion of a dead stillness as the striking of distant clocks causes it to appear the more intense and insupportable when the sound has ceased. He listened with strained attention, in the hope that some clock, lagging behind its fellows, had yet to strike – looking all the time into the profound darkness before him until it seemed to weave itself into a black tissue, patterned with a hundred reflections of his own eyes. But the bells had all pealed out their warning for that once, and the gust of wind that moaned through the place seemed cold and heavy with their iron breath.

The time and circumstances were favourable to reflection. He tried to keep his thoughts to the current, unpleasant though it was, in which they had moved all day, and to think with what a romantic feeling he had looked forward to shaking his old friend by the hand before he died, and what a wide and cruel difference there was between the meeting they had had, and that which he had so often and so long anticipated. Still, he was disordered by waking to such sudden loneliness, and could not prevent his mind from running upon odd tales of people of undoubted courage, who, being shut up by night in vaults or churches, or other dismal places, had scaled great heights to get out, and fled from silence as they had never done from danger. This brought to his mind the moonlight through the window, and bethinking himself of it, he groped his way back up the crooked stairs – but very stealthily, as though he were fearful of being overheard.

He was very much astonished when he approached the gallery again, to see a light in the building: still more so, on advancing hastily and looking round, to observe no visible source from which it could proceed. But how much greater yet was his astonishment at the spectacle which this light revealed!

The statues of the two giants, Gog and Magog, each above fourteen feet in height, those which succeeded to still older and more barbarous figures after the great fire of London, and which stand in the Guildhall to this day, were endowed with life and motion. These guardian genii of the city had quitted their pedestals, and reclined in easy attitudes in the great stained glass window. Between them was an ancient cask, which seemed to be full of wine; for the younger giant, clapping his huge hand upon it, and throwing up his mighty leg, burst into an exulting laugh, which reverberated through the hall like thunder.

Joe Toddyhigh instinctively stooped down, and, more dead than alive, felt his hair stand on end, his knees knock together, and a cold damp break out upon his forehead. But even at that minute curiosity prevailed over every other feeling, and, somewhat reassured by the good humour of the giants and their apparent unconsciousness of his presence, he crouched in a corner of the gallery, in as small a space as he could, and, peeping between the rails, observed them closely.

Turning toward his companion, the elder giant uttered these words in a grave majestic tone.

'Magog, does boisterous mirth beseem the Giant Warder of this ancient city? Is this becoming demeanour for a watchful spirit, over whose bodiless head so many years have rolled, so many changes swept like empty air – in whose impalpable nostrils the scent of blood and crime, pestilence, cruelty, and horror, has been familiar as breath to mortals – in whose sight Time has gathered in the harvest of centuries, and garnered so many crops of human pride, affections, hopes, and sorrows? Bethink you of our compact. The night wanes; feasting, revelry, and music have encroached upon our usual hours of solitude, and morning will be here apace. Ere we are stricken mute again, bethink you of our compact.'

Pronouncing these latter words with more of impatience than quite accorded with his apparent age and gravity, the giant raised a long pole (which he still bears in his hand) and tapped his brother giant rather smartly on the head; indeed, the blow was so smartly administered, that the latter quickly withdrew his lips from the cask, to which they had been applied, and, catching up his shield and halberd, assumed an attitude of defence. His irritation was but momentary, for he laid these weapons aside as hastily as he had assumed them, and said as he did so –

'You know, Gog, old friend, that when we animate these shapes which the Londoners of old assigned (and not unworthily) to the guardian genii of their city, we are susceptible of some of the sensations which belong to human kind. Thus, when I taste wine I feel blows; when I relish the one, I disrelish the other. Therefore, Gog, the more especially as your arm is none of the lightest, keep your good staff by your side, else we may chance to differ. Peace be between us.'

'Amen!' said the other, leaning his staff in the window-corner. 'Why did you laugh just now?'

'To think,' replied the Giant Magog, laying his hand upon the cask, 'of him who owned this wine, and kept it in a cellar hoarded from the light of day, for thirty years, "till it should be fit to drink", quoth he. He was two score and ten years old when he buried it beneath his house, and yet never thought that he might be scarcely "fit to drink" when the wine became so. I wonder it never occurred to him to make himself unfit to be eaten. There is very little of him left by this time.'

'The night is waning,' said Gog, mournfully.

'I know it,' replied his companion, 'and I see you are impatient. But look. Through the eastern window placed opposite to us, that the first beams of the rising sun may every morning gild our giant faces – the moon-rays fall upon the pavement in a stream of light that to my fancy sinks through the cold stone and gushes into the old crypt below. The night is scarcely past its noon, and our great charge is sleeping heavily.'

They ceased to speak, and looked upward at the moon. The sight of their large, black, rolling eyes filled Joe Toddyhigh with such horror that he could scarcely draw his breath. Still they took no note of him, and appeared to believe themselves quite alone.

'Our compact,' said Magog after a pause, 'is, if I understand it, that, instead of watching here in silence through the dreary nights, we entertain each other with stories of our past experience – with tales of the past, the present, and the future – with legends of London and her sturdy citizens from the old simple times. That every night at midnight, when St Paul's bell tolls out one, and we may move and speak, we thus discourse, nor leave such themes till the first gray gleam of day shall strike us dumb. Is that our bargain, brother?'

'Yes,' said the giant Gog, 'that is the league between us who guard this city, by day in spirit, and by night in body also; and never on ancient holidays have its conduits run wine more merrily than we will pour forth our legendary lore. We are old chroniclers from this time hence. The crumbled walls encircle us once more, the postern-gates are closed, the drawbridge is up, and pent in its narrow den beneath, the water foams and struggles with the sunken starlings. Jerkins and quarter-staves are in the streets again, the nightly watch is set, the rebel, sad and lonely in his Tower dungeon, tries to sleep, and weeps for home and children. Aloft upon the gates and walls are noble heads, glaring fiercely down upon the dreaming city, and vexing the hungry dogs that scent them in the air, and tear the ground beneath with dismal howlings. The axe, the block, the rack, in their dark chambers give signs of recent use. The Thames, floating past long lines of cheerful windows whence come a burst of music and a stream of light, bears sullenly to the palace wall the last red stain brought on the tide from Traitor's gate. But your pardon, brother. The night wears, and I am talking idly.'

The other giant appeared to be entirely of this opinion, for, during the foregoing rhapsody of his fellow-sentinel, he had been scratching his head with an air of comical uneasiness, or rather with an air that would have been very comical if he had been a dwarf or an ordinary-sized man. He winked too, and though it could not be doubted for a moment that he winked to himself, still he certainly cocked his enormous eye towards the gallery where the listener was concealed. Nor was this all, for he gaped; and when he gaped, Joe was horribly reminded of the popular prejudice on the subject of giants, and of their fabled power of smelling out Englishmen, however closely concealed.

His alarm was such that he nearly swooned, and it was some little time before his power of sight or hearing was restored. When he recovered he found that the elder giant was pressing the younger to commence the chronicles, and that the latter was endeavouring to excuse himself on the ground that the night was far spent, and it would be better to wait until the next. Well assured by this that he was certainly about to begin directly, the listener collected his faculties by a great effort, and distinctly heard Magog express himself to the following effect:

In the sixteenth century and in the reign of Queen Elizabeth of glorious memory (albeit her golden days are sadly rusted with blood), there lived in the city of London a bold young prentice who loved his master's daughter. There were, no doubt, within the walls a great many prentices in this condition, but I speak of only one, and his name was Hugh Graham.

This Hugh was apprenticed to an honest Bowyer, who dwelt in the ward of Cheype, and was rumoured to possess great wealth. Rumour was quite as infallible in those days as at the present time, but it happened then, as now, to be sometimes right by accident. It stumbled upon the truth when it gave the old Bowyer a mint of money. His trade had been a profitable one in the time of King Henry the Eighth, who encouraged English archery to the utmost, and he had been prudent and discreet. Thus it came to pass that Mistress Alice, his only daughter, was the richest heiress in all his wealthy ward. Young Hugh had often maintained with staff and cudgel that she was the handsomest. To do him justice, I believe she was.

If he could have gained the heart of pretty Mistress Alice by knocking this conviction into stubborn people's heads, Hugh would have had no cause to fear. But though the Bowyer's daughter smiled in secret to hear of his doughty deeds for her sake, and though her little waiting woman reported all her smiles (and many more) to Hugh, and though he was at a vast expense in kisses and small coin to recompense her fidelity, he made no progress in his love. He durst not whisper it to Mistress Alice save on sure encouragement, and that she never gave him. A glance of her dark eye, as she sat at the door on a summer's evening after prayer-time, while he and the neighbouring prentices exercised themselves in the street with blunted sword and buckler, would fire Hugh's blood so that none could stand before him; but then, she glanced at others quite as kindly as on him, and where was the use of cracking crowns if Mistress Alice smiled upon the cracked as well as on the cracker?

Still Hugh went on, and loved her more and more. He thought of her all day, and dreamed of her all night long. He treasured up her every word and gesture, and had a palpitation of the heart whenever he heard her footstep on the stairs or her voice in an adjoining room. To him, the old Bowyer's house was haunted by an angel; there was enchantment in the air and space in which she moved. It would have been no miracle to Hugh if flowers had sprung from the rush-strewn floors beneath the tread of lovely Mistress Alice.

Never did prentice long to distinguish himself in the eyes of his lady-love so ardently as Hugh. Sometimes he pictured to himself the house taking fire by night, and he, when all drew back in fear, rushing through flame and smoke, and bearing her from the ruins in his arms. At other times he thought of a rising of fierce rebels, an attack upon the city, a strong assault upon the Bowyer's house in particular, and he falling on the threshold, pierced with numberless wounds in defence of Mistress Alice. If he could only enact some prodigy of valour, do some wonderful deed, and let her know that she had inspired it, he thought he could die contented.

Sometimes the Bowyer and his daughter would go out to supper with a worthy citizen at the fashionable hour of six o'clock, and on such occasions Hugh, wearing his blue prentice cloak as gallantly as prentice might, would attend with a lantern and his trusty club to escort them home. These were the brightest moments of his life. To hold the light while Mistress Alice picked her steps, to touch her hand as he helped her over broken ways, to have her leaning on his arm – it sometimes even came to that – this was happiness indeed!

When the nights were fair Hugh followed in the rear, his eyes riveted on the graceful figure of the Bowyer's daughter as she and the old man moved on before him. So they threaded the narrow winding streets of the city, now passing beneath the overhanging gables of old wooden houses whence creaking signs projected into the street, and now emerging from some dark and frowning gateway into the clear moonlight. At such times, or when the shouts of straggling brawlers met her ear, the Bowyer's daughter would look timidly back at Hugh, beseeching him to draw nearer; and then how he grasped his club and longed to do battle with a dozen rufflers, for the love of Mistress Alice!

The old Bowyer was in the habit of lending money on interest to the gallants of the court, and thus it happened that many a richly dressed gentleman dismounted at his door. More waving plumes and gallant steeds, indeed, were seen at the Bowyer's house, and more embroidered silks and velvets sparkled in his dark shop and darker private closet, than at any merchants in the city. In those times no less than in the present it would seem that the richest-looking cavaliers often wanted money the most.

Of these glittering clients there was one who always came alone. He was nobly mounted, and, having no attendant, gave his horse in charge to Hugh while he and the Bowyer were closeted within. Once as he sprung into the saddle Mistress Alice was seated at an upper window, and before she could withdraw he had doffed his jewelled cap and kissed his hand. Hugh watched him caracoling down the street, and burnt with indignation. But how much deeper was the glow that reddened in his cheeks when, raising his eyes to the casement, he saw that Alice watched the stranger too!

He came again and often, each time arrayed more gaily than before, and still the little casement showed him Mistress Alice. At length one heavy day, she fled from home. It had cost her a hard struggle, for all her old father's gifts were strewn about her chamber as if she had parted from them one by one, and knew that the time must come when these tokens of his love would wring her heart – yet she was gone.

She left a letter commanding her poor father to the care of Hugh, and wishing he might be happier than ever he could have been with her, for he deserved the love of a better and a purer heart than she had to bestow. The old man's forgiveness (she said) she had no power to ask, but she prayed God to bless him – and so ended with a blot upon the paper where her tears had fallen.

At first the old man's wrath was kindled, and he carried his wrong to the Queen's throne itself; but there was no redress he learnt at court, for his daughter had been conveyed abroad. This afterwards appeared to be the truth, as there came from France, after an interval of several years, a letter in her hand. It was written in trembling characters, and almost illegible. Little could be made out save that she often thought of home and her old dear pleasant room – and that she had dreamt her father was dead and had not blessed her – and that her heart was breaking.

The poor old Bowyer lingered on, never suffering Hugh to quit his sight, for he knew now that he had loved his daughter, and that was the only link that bound him to earth. It broke at length and he died, bequeathing his old prentice his trade and all his wealth, and solemnly charging him, with his last breath, to revenge his child if ever he who had worked her misery crossed his path in life again.

From the time of Alice's flight, the tilting-ground, the fields, the fencing-school, the summer evening sports, knew Hugh no more. His spirit was dead within him. He rose to great eminence and repute among the citizens, but he was never seen to smile, and never mingled in their revelries or rejoicings. Brave, humane, and generous, he was loved by all. He was pitied too by those who knew his story, and these were so many, that, when he walked along the streets alone at dusk, even the rude common people doffed their caps and mingled a rough air of sympathy with their respect.

One night in May – it was her birth-night, and twenty years since she had left her home – Hugh Graham sat in the room she had hallowed in his boyish days. He was now a grey-haired man, though still in the prime of life. Old thoughts had borne him company for many hours, and the chamber had gradually grown quite dark, when he was roused by a low knocking at the outer door.

He hastened down, and opening it, saw by the light of a lamp, which he had seized upon the way, a female figure crouching in the portal. It hurried swiftly past him and glided up the stairs. He looked for pursuers. There were none in sight.

He was inclined to think it a vision of his own brain, when suddenly a vague suspicion of the truth flashed upon his mind. He barred the door, and hastened wildly back. Yes, there she was – there, in the chamber he had quitted – there, in her old innocent, happy home, so changed that none but he could trace one gleam of what she had been – there upon her knees – with her hands clasped in agony and shame before her burning face.

'My God, my God!' she cried, 'now strike me dead! Though I have brought death and shame and sorrow on this roof, oh, let me die at home in mercy!'

There was no tear upon her face then, but she trembled and glanced round the chamber. Everything was in its old place. Her bed looked as if she had risen from it but that morning. The sight of these familiar objects, marking the dear remembrance in which she had been held, and the blight she had brought upon herself, was more than the woman's better nature that had carried her there could bear. She wept and fell upon the ground.

A rumour was spread about, in a few days' time, that the Bowyer's cruel daughter had come home, and that Master Graham had given her lodging in his house. It was rumoured, too, that he had resigned her fortune, in order that she might bestow it in acts of charity, and that he had vowed to guard her in her solitude, but that they were never to see each other more. These rumours greatly incensed all virtuous wives and daughters in the ward, especially when they appeared to receive some corroboration from the circumstance of Master Graham taking up his abode in another tenement hard by. The estimation in which he was held, however, forbade any questioning on the subject; and as the Bowyer's house was close shut up, and nobody came forth when public shows and festivities were in progress, or to flaunt in the public walks, or to buy new fashions at the mercers' booths, all the well-conducted females agreed among themselves that there could be no woman there.

These reports had scarcely died away when the wonder of every good citizen, male and female, was utterly absorbed and swallowed up by a royal proclamation, in which Her Majesty, strongly censuring the practice of wearing long Spanish rapiers of preposterous length (as being a bullying and swaggering custom, tending to bloodshed and public disorder), commanded that on a particular day therein named certain grave citizens should repair to the city gates, and there, in public, break all rapiers worn or carried by persons claiming admission, that exceeded, though it were only by a quarter of an inch, three standard feet in length.

Royal proclamations usually take their course, let the public wonder never so much. On the appointed day two citizens of high repute took up their stations at each of the gates, attended by a party of the city guard: the main body to enforce the Queen's will, and take custody of all such rebels (if any) as might have the temerity to dispute it: and a few to bear the standard measures and instruments for reducing all unlawful sword-blades to the prescribed dimensions. In pursuance of these arrangements, Master Graham and another were posted at Ludgate, on the hill before St Paul's.

A pretty numerous company were gathered together at this spot, for, besides the officers in attendance to enforce the proclamation, there was a motley crowd of lookers-on of various degrees, who raised from time to time such shouts and cries as the circumstances called forth. A spruce young courtier was the first who approached; he unsheathed a weapon of burnished steel that shone and glistened in the sun, and handed it with the newest air to the officer, who, finding it exactly three feet long, returned it with a bow. Thereupon the gallant raised his hat and crying, 'God save the Queen,' passed on amidst the plaudits of the mob. Then came another – a better courtier still – who wore a blade but two feet long, whereat the people laughed, much to the disparagement of his honour's dignity. Then came a third, a sturdy old officer of the army, girded with a rapier at least a foot and a half beyond Her Majesty's pleasure; at him they raised a great shout, and most of the spectators (but especially those who were armourers or cutlers) laughed very heartily at the breakage which would ensue. But they were disappointed, for the old campaigner, coolly unbuckling his sword and bidding his servant carry it home again, passed through unarmed, to the great indignation of all the spectators. They relieved themselves in some degree by hooting a tall blustering fellow with a prodigious weapon, who stopped short on coming in sight of the preparations, and after a little consideration turned back again; but all this time no rapier had been broken, although it was high noon, and all cavaliers of any quality or appearance were taking their way towards St Paul's churchyard.

During these proceedings, Master Graham had stood apart, strictly confining himself to the duty imposed upon him, and taking little heed of anything beyond. He stepped forward now, as a richly dressed gentleman on foot, followed by a single attendant, was seen advancing up the hill.

As this person drew nearer, the crowd stopped their clamour, and bent forward with eager looks. Master Graham standing alone in the gateway, and the stranger coming slowly towards him, they seemed, as it were, set face to face. The nobleman (for he looked one) had a haughty and disdainful air, which bespoke the slight estimation in which he held the citizen. The citizen, on the other hand, preserved the resolute bearing of one who was not to be frowned down or daunted, and who cared very little for any nobility but that of worth and manhood. It was perhaps some consciousness on the part of each, of these feelings in the other, that infused a more stern expression into their regards as they came closer together.

'Your rapier, worthy sir!'

At the instant that he pronounced these words Graham started, and falling back some paces, laid his hand upon the dagger in his belt.

'You are the man whose horse I used to hold before the Bowyer's door? You are that man? Speak!'

'Out, you prentice hound!' said the other.

'You are he! I know you well!' cried Graham. 'Let no man step between us two, or I shall be his murderer.' With that he drew his dagger, and rushed in upon him.

The stranger had drawn his weapon from the scabbard ready for the scrutiny, before a word was spoken. He made a thrust at his assailant, but the dagger which Graham clutched in his left hand being the dirk in use at that time for parrying such blows, promptly turned the point aside. They closed. The dagger fell rattling on the ground, and Graham, wresting his adversary's sword from his grasp, plunged it through his heart. As he drew it out it snapped in two, leaving a fragment in the dead man's body.

All this passed so swiftly that the bystanders looked on without an effort to interfere; but the man was no sooner down than an uproar broke forth which rent the air. The attendant, rushing through the gate, proclaimed that his master, a nobleman, had been set upon and slain by a citizen; the word quickly spread from mouth to mouth; St Paul's cathedral, and every bookshop, ordinary, and smoking-house in the churchyard poured out its stream of cavaliers and their followers, who, mingling together in a dense tumultuous body, struggled, sword in hand, towards the spot.

With equal impetuosity, and stimulating each other by loud cries and shouts, the citizens and common people took up the quarrel on their side, and encircling Master Graham a hundred deep, forced him from the gate. In vain he waved the broken sword above his head, crying that he would die on London's threshold for their sacred homes. They bore him on, and ever keeping him in the midst, so that no man could attack him, fought their way into the city.

The clash of swords and roar of voices, the dust and heat and pressure, the trampling under foot of men, the distracted looks and shrieks of women at the windows above as they recognised their relatives or lovers in the crowd, the rapid tolling of alarm bells, the furious rage and passion of the scene, were fearful.

Those who, being on the outskirts of each crowd, could use their weapons with effect fought desperately, while those behind, maddened with baffled rage, struck at each other over the heads of those before them, and crushed their own fellows. Wherever the broken sword was seen above the people's heads, towards that spot the cavaliers made a new rush. Every one of these charges was marked by sudden gaps in the throng where men were trodden down; but as fast as they were made, the tide swept over them, and still the multitude pressed on again, a confused mass of swords, clubs, staves, broken plumes, fragments of rich cloaks and doublets, and angry, bleeding faces, all mixed up together in inextricable disorder.

The design of the people was to force Master Graham to take refuge in his dwelling, and to defend it until the authorities could interfere or they could gain time for parley. But either from ignorance, or in the confusion of the moment, they stopped at his old house, which was closely shut. Some time was lost in beating the doors open and passing him to the front. About a score of the boldest of the other party threw themselves into the torrent while this was being done, and reaching the door at the same moment with himself cut him off from his defenders.

'I never will turn in such a righteous cause, so help me Heaven!' cried Graham, in a voice that at last made itself heard, and confronting them as he spoke. 'Least of all will I turn upon this threshold which owes its desolation to such men as ye. I give no quarter, and I will have none! Strike!'

For a moment they stood at bay. At that moment a shot from an unseen hand – apparently fired by some person who had gained access to one of the opposite houses – struck Graham in the brain, and he fell dead. A low wail was heard in the air; many people in the concourse cried that they had seen a spirit glide across the little casement window of the Bowyer's house.

A dead silence succeeded. After a short time some of the flushed and heated throng laid down their arms and softly carried the body within doors. Others fell off or slunk away in knots of two or three, others whispered together in groups, and before a numerous guard which then rode up, could muster in the street, it was nearly empty.

Those who carried Master Graham to the bed upstairs were shocked to see a woman lying beneath the window with her hands clasped together. After trying to recover her in vain, they laid her near the citizen, who still retained, tightly grasped in his right hand, the first and last sword that was broken that day at Ludgate.

The giant uttered these concluding words with sudden precipitation; and on the instant the strange light which had filled the hall faded away. Joe glanced involuntarily at the eastern window, and saw the first pale gleam of morning. He turned his head again towards the other window in which the giants had been seated. It was empty. The cask of wine was gone, and he could dimly make out that the two great figures stood mute and motionless upon their pedestals.

After rubbing his eyes and wondering for full half an hour, during which time he observed morning come creeping on, he yielded to the drowsiness which overpowered him and fell into a refreshing slumber. When he awoke it was broad day; the building was open, and workmen were busily engaged in removing the vestiges of last night's feast.

Stealing gently down the little stairs, and assuming the air of some early lounger who had dropped in from the street, he walked up to the foot of each pedestal in turn, and attentively examined the figure it supported. There could be no doubt about the features of either; he recollected the exact expression they had worn at different passages of their conversation, and recognised in every line and lineament the giants of the night. Assured that it was no vision, but that he had heard and seen with his own proper senses, he walked forth, determining at all hazards to conceal himself in the Guildhall again that evening. He farther resolved to sleep all day, so that he might be very wakeful and vigilant, and above all that he might take notice of the figures at the precise moment of their becoming animated and subsiding into their old state, which he greatly reproached himself for not having done already.

Night Walks

Some years ago, a temporary inability to sleep, referable to a distressing impression,[19] caused me to walk about the streets all night, for a series of several nights. The disorder might have taken a long time to conquer, if it had been faintly experimented on in bed; but, it was soon defeated by the brisk treatment of getting up directly after lying down, and going out, and coming home tired at sunrise.

In the course of those nights, I finished my education in a fair amateur experience of houselessness. My principal object being to get through the night, the pursuit of it brought me into sympathetic relations with people who have no other object every night in the year.

The month was March, and the weather damp, cloudy, and cold. The sun not rising before half-past five, the night perspective looked sufficiently long at half-past twelve: which was about my time for confronting it.

The restlessness of a great city, and the way in which it tumbles and tosses before it can get to sleep, formed one of the first entertainments offered to the contemplation of us houseless people. It lasted about two hours. We lost a great deal of companionship when the late public houses turned their lamps out, and when the potmen thrust the last brawling drunkards into the street; but stray vehicles and stray people were left us, after that. If we were very lucky, a policeman's rattle sprang and a fray turned up; but, in general, surprisingly little of this diversion was provided. Except in the Haymarket, which is the worst kept part of London, and about Kent Street in the Borough, and along a portion of the line of the Old Kent Road, the peace was seldom violently broken. But, it was always the case that London, as if in imitation of individual citizens belonging to it, had expiring fits and starts of restlessness. After all seemed quiet, if one cab rattled by, half a dozen would surely follow; and

Houselessness even observed that intoxicated people appeared to be magnetically attracted towards each other; so that we knew when we saw one drunken object staggering against the shutters of a shop, that another drunken object would stagger up before five minutes were out, to fraternise or fight with it. When we made a divergence from the regular species of drunkard, the thin-armed puff-faced leaden-lipped gin-drinker, and encountered a rarer specimen of a more decent appearance, fifty to one but that specimen was dressed in soiled mourning. As the street experience in the night, so the street experience in the day; the common folk who come unexpectedly into a little property, come unexpectedly into a deal of liquor.

At length these flickering sparks would die away, worn out – the last veritable sparks of waking life trailed from some late pie-man or hot-potato man – and London would sink to rest. And then the yearning of the houseless mind would be for any sign of company, any lighted place, any movement, anything suggestive of any one being up – nay, even so much as awake, for the houseless eye looked out for lights in windows.

Walking the streets under the pattering rain, Houselessness would walk and walk and walk, seeing nothing but the interminable tangle of streets, save at a corner, here and there, two policemen in conversation, or the sergeant or inspector looking after his men. Now and then in the night – but rarely – Houselessness would become aware of a furtive head peering out of a doorway a few yards before him, and, coming up with the head, would find a man standing bolt upright to keep within the doorway's shadow, and evidently intent upon no particular service to society. Under a kind of fascination, and in a ghostly silence suitable to the time, Houselessness and this gentleman would eye one another from head to foot, and so, without exchange of speech, part, mutually suspicious. Drip, drip, drip, from ledge and coping, splash from pipes and water-spouts, and by-and-by the houseless shadow would fall upon the stones that pave the way to Waterloo Bridge; it being in the houseless mind to have a halfpenny worth of excuse for saying 'Good night' to the toll-keeper, and catching a glimpse of his fire. A good fire and a good great-coat and a good woollen neck-shawl, were comfortable things to see in conjunction with the toll-keeper; also his brisk wakefulness was excellent company when he rattled the change of halfpence down upon that metal table of his, like a man who defied the night, with all its sorrowful thoughts, and didn't care for the coming of dawn. There was need of encouragement on the threshold of the bridge, for the bridge was dreary. The chopped up murdered man, had not been lowered with a rope over the parapet when those nights were;[20] he was alive, and slept then quietly enough most likely, and undisturbed by any dream of where he was to come. But the river had an awful look, the buildings on the banks were muffled in black shrouds, and the reflected lights seemed to originate deep in the water, as if the spectres of suicides were holding them to show where they went down. The wild moon and clouds were as restless as an evil conscience in a tumbled bed, and the very shadow of the immensity of London seemed to lie oppressively upon the river.

Between the bridge and the two great theatres, there was but the distance of a few hundred paces, so the theatres came next. Grim and black within, at night, those great dry Wells, and lonesome to imagine, with the rows of faces faded out, the lights extinguished, and the seats all empty. One would think that nothing in them knew itself at such a time but Yorick's skull. In one of my night walks, as the church steeples were shaking the March winds and rain with the strokes of four, I passed the outer boundary of one of these great deserts, and entered it. With a dim lantern in my hand, I groped my well-known way to the stage and looked over the orchestra – which was like a great grave dug for a time of pestilence – into the void beyond. A dismal cavern of an immense aspect, with the chandelier gone dead like everything else, and nothing visible through mist and fog and space, but tiers of winding-sheets. The ground at my feet where, when last there, I had seen the peasantry of Naples dancing among the vines, reckless of the burning mountain which threatened to overwhelm them, was now in possession of a strong serpent of engine-hose, watchfully lying in wait for the serpent Fire, and ready to fly at it if it showed its forked tongue. A ghost of a watchman, carrying a faint corpse candle, haunted the distant upper gallery and flitted away. Retiring within the proscenium, and holding my light above my head towards the rolled-up curtain – green no more, but black as ebony – my sight lost itself in a gloomy vault, showing faint indications in it of a shipwreck of canvas and cordage. Methought I felt much as a diver might, at the bottom of the sea.

In those small hours when there was no movement in the streets, it afforded matter for reflection to take Newgate in the way, and, touching its rough stone, to think of the prisoners in their sleep, and then to glance in at the lodge over the spiked wicket, and see the fire and light of the watching turnkeys, on the white wall. Not an inappropriate time either, to linger by that wicked little debtors' door – shutting tighter than any other door one ever saw – which has been death's door to so many. In the days of the uttering of forged one-pound notes by people tempted up from the country, how many hundreds of wretched creatures of both sexes – many quite innocent – swung out of a pitiless and inconsistent world, with the tower of yonder Christian church of Saint Sepulchre monstrously before their eyes! Is there any haunting of the bank parlour, by the remorseful souls of old directors, in the nights of these later days, I wonder, or is it as quiet as this degenerate Aceldama of an Old Bailey?

To walk on to the Bank, lamenting the good old times and bemoaning the present evil period, would be an easy next step, so I would take it, and would make my houseless circuit of the Bank, and give a thought to the treasure within; likewise to the guard of soldiers passing the night there, and nodding over the fire. Next, I went to Billingsgate, in some hope of market-people, but it proving as yet too early, crossed London Bridge and got down by the water-side on the Surrey shore among the buildings of the great brewery. There was plenty going on at the brewery; and the reek, and the smell of grains, and the rattling of the plump dray horses at their mangers, were capital company. Quite refreshed by having mingled with this good society, I made a new start with a new heart, setting the old King's Bench prison before me for my next object, and resolving, when I should come to the wall, to think of poor Horace Kinch, and the Dry Rot in men.

A very curious disease the Dry Rot in men, and difficult to detect the beginning of. It had carried Horace Kinch inside the wall of the old King's Bench prison, and it had carried him out with his feet foremost. He was a likely man to look at, in the prime of life, well to do, as clever as he needed to be, and popular among many friends. He was suitably married, and had healthy and pretty children. But, like some fair-looking houses or fair-looking ships, he took the Dry Rot. The first strong external revelation of the Dry Rot in men, is a tendency to lurk and lounge; to be at street-corners without intelligible reason; to be going anywhere when met; to be about many places rather than at any; to do nothing tangible, but to have an intention of performing a variety of intangible duties tomorrow or the day after. When this manifestation of the disease is observed, the observer will usually connect it with a vague impression once formed or received, that the patient was living a little too hard. He will scarcely have had leisure to turn it over in his mind and form the terrible suspicion 'Dry Rot', when he will notice a change for the worse in the patient's appearance: a certain slovenliness and deterioration, which is not poverty, nor dirt, nor intoxication, nor ill-health, but simply Dry Rot. To this, succeeds a smell as of strong waters, in the morning; to that, a looseness respecting money; to that, a stronger smell as of strong waters, at all times; to that, a looseness respecting everything; to that, a trembling of the limbs, somnolency, misery, and crumbling to pieces. As it is in wood, so it is in men. Dry Rot advances at a compound usury quite incalculable. A plank is found infected with it, and the whole structure is devoted. Thus it had been with the unhappy Horace Kinch, lately buried by a small subscription. Those who knew him had not nigh done saying, 'So well off, so comfortably established, with such hope before him and yet, it is feared, with a slight touch of Dry Rot!' when lo! the man was all Dry Rot and dust.

From the dead wall associated on those houseless nights with this too common story, I chose next to wander by Bethlehem Hospital; partly, because it lay on my road round to Westminster; partly, because I had a night fancy in my head which could be best pursued within sight of its walls and dome. And the fancy was this: Are not the sane and the insane equal at night as the sane lie a dreaming? Are not all of us outside this hospital, who dream, more or less in the condition of those inside it, every night of our lives? Are we not nightly persuaded, as they daily are, that we associate preposterously with kings and queens, emperors and empresses, and notabilities of all sorts? Do we not nightly jumble events and personages and times and places, as these do daily? Are we not sometimes troubled by our own sleeping inconsistencies, and do we not vexedly try to account for them or excuse them, just as these do sometimes in respect of their waking delusions? Said an afflicted man to me, when I was last in a hospital like this, 'Sir, I can frequently fly.' I was half ashamed to reflect that so could I – by night. Said a woman to me on the same occasion, 'Queen Victoria frequently comes to dine with me, and Her Majesty and I dine off peaches and maccaroni in our nightgowns, and his Royal Highness the Prince Consort does us the honour to make a third on horseback in a Field Marshal's uniform.' Could I refrain from reddening with consciousness when I remembered the amazing royal parties I myself had given (at night), the unaccountable viands I had put on table, and my extraordinary manner of conducting myself on those distinguished occasions? I wonder that the great master who knew everything, when he called sleep the death of each day's life, did not call dreams the insanity of each day's sanity.

By this time I had left the hospital behind me, and was again setting towards the river; and in a short breathing space I was on Westminster Bridge, regaling my houseless eyes with the external walls of the British Parliament – the perfection of a stupendous institution, I know, and the admiration of all surrounding nations and succeeding ages, I do not doubt, but perhaps a little the better now and then for being pricked up to its work. Turning off into Old Palace Yard, the Courts of Law kept me company for a quarter of an hour, hinting in low whispers what numbers of people they were keeping awake, and how intensely wretched and horrible they were rendering the small hours to unfortunate suitors. Westminster Abbey was fine gloomy society for another quarter of an hour; suggesting a wonderful procession of its dead among the dark arches and pillars, each century more amazed by the century following it than by all the centuries going before. And indeed in those houseless night walks – which even included cemeteries where watchmen went round among the graves at stated times, and moved the tell-tale handle of an index which recorded that they had touched it at such an hour – it was a solemn consideration what enormous hosts of dead belong to one old great city, and how, if they were raised while the living slept, there would not be the space of a pin's point in all the streets and ways for the living to come out into. Not only that, but the vast armies of dead would overflow the hills and valleys beyond the city, and would stretch away all round it, God knows how far.

When a church clock strikes, on houseless ears in the dead of the night, it may be at first mistaken for company and hailed as such. But, as the spreading circles of vibration, which you may perceive at such a time with great clearness, go opening out, for ever and ever afterwards widening perhaps (as the philosopher has suggested) in eternal space, the mistake is rectified and the sense of loneliness is profounder. Once – it was after leaving the Abbey and turning my face north – I came to the great steps of St Martin's church as the clock was striking three. Suddenly, a thing that in a moment more I should have trodden upon without seeing, rose up at my feet with a cry of loneliness and houseless-ness, struck out of it by the bell, the like of which I never heard. We then stood face to face looking at one another, frightened by one another. The creature was like a beetle-browed hare-lipped youth of twenty, and it had a loose bundle of rags on, which it held together with one of its hands. It shivered from head to foot, and its teeth chattered, and as it stared at me – persecutor, devil, ghost, whatever it thought me – it made with its whining mouth as if it were snapping at me, like a worried dog. Intending to give this ugly object money, I put out my hand to stay it – for it recoiled as it whined and snapped – and laid my hand upon its shoulder. Instantly, it twisted out of its garment, like the young man in the New Testament,[21] and left me standing alone with its rags in my hands.

Covent Garden Market, when it was market morning, was wonderful company. The great wagons of cabbages, with growers' men and boys lying asleep under them, and with sharp dogs from market-garden neighbourhoods looking after the whole, were as good as a party. But one of the worst night sights I know in London, is to be found in the children who prowl about this place; who sleep in the baskets, fight for the offal, dart at any object they think they can lay their thieving hands on, dive under the carts and barrows, dodge the constables, and are perpetually making a blunt pattering on the pavement of the Piazza with the rain of their naked feet. A painful and unnatural result comes of the comparison one is forced to institute between the growth of corruption as displayed in the so-much-improved and cared-for fruits of the earth, and the growth of corruption as displayed in these all uncared-for (except inasmuch as ever-hunted) savages.

There was early coffee to be got about Covent Garden Market, and that was more company – warm company, too, which was better. Toast of a very substantial quality, was likewise procurable: though the towzled-headed man who made it, in an inner chamber within the coffee room, hadn't got his coat on yet, and was so heavy with sleep that in every interval of toast and coffee he went off anew behind the partition into complicated crossroads of choke and snore, and lost his way directly. Into one of these establishments (among the earliest) near Bow Street, there came one morning as I sat over my houseless cup, pondering where to go next, a man in a high and long snuff-coloured coat, and shoes, and, to the best of my belief, nothing else but a hat, who took out of his hat a large cold meat pudding; a meat pudding so large that it was a very tight fit, and brought the lining of the hat out with it. This mysterious man was known by his pudding, for on his entering, the man of sleep brought him a pint of hot tea, a small loaf, and a large knife and fork and plate. Left to himself in his box, he stood the pudding on the bare table, and, instead of cutting it, stabbed it, overhand, with the knife, like a mortal enemy; then took the knife out, wiped it on his sleeve, tore the pudding asunder with his fingers, and ate it all up. The remembrance of this man with the pudding remains with me as the remembrance of the most spectral person my houselessness encountered. Twice only was I in that establishment, and twice I saw him stalk in (as I should say, just out of bed, and presently going back to bed), take out his pudding, stab his pudding, wipe the dagger, and eat his pudding all up. He was a man whose figure promised cadaverousness, but who had an excessively red face, though shaped like a horse's. On the second occasion of my seeing him, he said huskily to the man of sleep, 'Am I red tonight?' 'You are,' he uncompromisingly answered. 'My mother,' said the spectre, 'was a red-faced woman that liked drink, and I looked at her hard when she laid in her coffin, and I took the complexion.' Somehow, the pudding seemed an unwholesome pudding after that, and I put myself in its way no more.

When there was no market, or when I wanted variety, a railway terminus with the morning mails coming in was remunerative company. But like most of the company to be had in this world, it lasted only a very short time. The station lamps would burst out ablaze, the porters would emerge from places of concealment, the cabs and trucks would rattle to their places (the post-office carts were already in theirs), and, finally, the bell would strike up, and the train would come banging in. But there were few passengers and little luggage, and everything scuttled away with the greatest expedition. The locomotive post-offices, with their great nets – as if they had been dragging the country for bodies – would fly open as to their doors, and would disgorge a smell of lamp, an exhausted clerk, a guard in a red coat, and their bags of letters; the engine would blow and heave and perspire, like an engine wiping its forehead and saying what a run it had had; and within ten minutes the lamps were out, and I was houseless and alone again.

But now, there were driven cattle on the high road near, wanting (as cattle always do) to turn into the midst of stone walls, and squeeze themselves through six inches' width of iron railing, and getting their heads down (also as cattle always do) for tossing-purchase at quite imaginary dogs, and giving themselves and every devoted creature associated with them a most extraordinary amount of unnecessary trouble. Now, too, the conscious gas began to grow pale with the knowledge that daylight was coming, and straggling workpeople were already in the streets, and, as waking life had become extinguished with the last pieman's sparks, so it began to be rekindled with the fires of the first street-corner breakfast-sellers. And so by faster and faster degrees, until the last degrees were very fast, the day came, and I was tired and could sleep. And it is not, as I used to think, going home at such times, the least wonderful thing in London, that in the real desert region of the night, the houseless wanderer is alone there. I knew well enough where to find vice and misfortune of all kinds, if I had chosen; but they were put out of sight, and my houselessness had many miles upon miles of streets in which it could, and did, have its own solitary way.

Notes

1. Bampfylde Moore Carew was an eighteenth-century rogue who claimed to be king of the beggars.
2. It was traditional for the godfather to present the child with half a crown.
3. George Hudson, 'The Railway King', was publicly disgraced after being exposed for embezzlement; the scandal inspired the character of Mr Merdle in *Little Dorrit*.
4. In the story of Dick Whittington, Mr Fitzwarren is the kindly merchant who takes Dick in off the street.
5. Not the Scottish author, but a nineteenth-century politician and director of the East India company.
6. The New Shot Mill was built near Waterloo Bridge in 1826 and was considered something of an eyesore.
7. Standard measures of coal.
8. Reference to a contemporary comic piece *Monsieur Tonson* by John Taylor, in turn based on the real pranks of the actor Tom King who mischievously disturbed the home of a French couple each night by asking for a nonexistent Mr Thompson.
9. Catnach and Pitts were both printers of ballads.
10. Giovanni Belzoni (1778–1823) was a celebrated explorer.
11. A baked jemmy is a baked sheep's head.
12. John Byrne Leicester Warren, or the Baron de Tabley, was a poet with numerous pseudonyms.
13. A gin-based cocktail.
14. The real identity of Saint Ghastly Grim is St Olave's.
15. A turncock controlled the water supply; the fireplug he wrenches is a hydrant.
16. In the Arabian Nights, Aladdin finds the lamp in a vast subterranean area.
17. One of the chief auction houses in London, by Dickens' time it was an address for various merchants and brokers.
18. A guild of patten-makers, a patten being an undershoe to raise ordinary shoes above the mud.
19. Refers to the death of Dickens' father in March 1851, after which Dickens went on a number of nocturnal walks.
20. This chopped-up corpse was found by police on Waterloo Bridge in 1857.
21. Mark 14: 51–52: 'And there followed him a certain young man, having a linen cloth cast about his naked body; and the young men laid hold on him: And he left the linen cloth, and fled from them naked.'

Biographical note

Charles Dickens (1812–70), a true celebrity in the Victorian period, remains one of the best-known British writers. His most popular works, such as *Great Expectations* (1861) and *A Christmas Carol* (1843), continue to be read and adapted worldwide. In addition to fourteen complete novels, Dickens wrote short stories, essays, and plays.

At the age of ten, Dickens moved with his family from Chatham to London. Though his travels would later take him abroad, most notably to America, his permanent home remained in the city for the duration of his life. His early life was financially and emotionally unstable, and when his father was imprisoned for debt, he was sent to work in a blacking factory, an experience that haunted his later fiction. He worked as an office-boy and court reporter before his *Sketches by Boz* (1836–7) brought his writing to the attention of the publishing house Chapman and Hall. After the success of *The Posthumous Papers of the Pickwick Club*, Dickens was able to found the journal *Bentley's Miscellany*, and from then on all his major novels were published as serial instalments in his own magazines.

After more than twenty years of marriage, in 1858, Dickens abruptly separated from his wife Catherine, mother of his ten children, in order to pursue a relationship with Ellen Ternan, a young actress. He died suddenly in 1870, leaving his novel, *The Mystery of Edwin Drood*, unfinished.

Pete Orford gained his PhD from the Shakespeare Institute for researching the modern reception of Shakespeare's history plays. Since then he has become embroiled in an academic *ménage à trois* with Shakespeare and Dickens, presenting papers at conferences on both writers, as well as publishing articles and books. He is the general editor of *Divining Thoughts: Future Directions in Shakespeare Studies* and has edited two collections of Dickens' writings for Hesperus Press, including *On Travel* (2009) and the forthcoming *On Theatre*.

HESPERUS PRESS

Hesperus Press, as suggested by the Latin motto, is committed to bringing near what is far – far both in space and time. Works written by the greatest authors, and unjustly neglected or simply little known in the English-speaking world, are made accessible through new translations and a completely fresh editorial approach. Through these classic works, the reader is introduced to the greatest writers from all times and all cultures.

For more information on Hesperus Press, please visit our website: **www.hesperuspress.com**

ET REMOTISSIMA PROPE